C0-AWD-037

Mark L. Henberger

4-6-79

BIRTH TO BIRTH

1

BIRTH TO BIRTH
The Life-Death Mystery

REV. GERALD P. RUANE

Photo Editor: Sister M. Gerarda, O.P.

ALBA · HOUSE   NEW · YORK

SOCIETY OF ST. PAUL, 2187 VICTORY BLVD., STATEN ISLAND, NEW YORK 10314

The Scriptural quotations in this publication are from the *New American Bible*, 1970, used herein by permission of the Confraternity of Christian Doctrine, copyright owner.

Photography: Joseph De Caro

Sister M. Gerarda, O.P. pages 4 and 18

Library of Congress Cataloging in Publication Data

Ruane, Gerald P
   Birth to birth.

   1. Death.   2. Life.   3. Consolation.   I. Title.
BT825 . R76   236' 1   75-40300
ISBN   0-8189-0326-0

Nihil Obstat:
Daniel V. Flynn, J.C.D.
Censor Librorum

Imprimatur:
✠ James P. Mahoney, D.D.
Vicar General, Archdiocese of New York
January 17, 1976

*The Nihil Obstat and Imprimatur
are a declaration that a book or pamphlet is considered
to be free from doctrinal or moral error. It is not implied that
those who have granted the Nihil Obstat and Imprimatur agree
with the contents, opinions or statements expressed.*

*Designed, printed and bound in the United States of
America by the Fathers and Brothers of the Society of St. Paul,
2187 Victory Boulevard, Staten Island, New York, 10314,
as part of their communications apostolate.*

2 3 4 5 6 7 8 9 (Current Printing: first digit).

© *Copyright 1976 by the Society of St. Paul*

To my parents, family, and friends, and to all others who have shared their thoughts and hearts with me in this undertaking.

PREFACE

Birth to Birth

Your life begins and ends with birth.

You are born to live, and yet to die someday. You are born to die, and yet live forevermore.

You have many births, but two are crucial. The first is that traumatic experience when you are expelled from your mother's womb, and slapped into breathing, yelling, struggling life. The second is equally traumatic; for by it you are torn from the womb of this life and plunged into the mysterious existence of the next life.

In each birth, *you* are born. You, unique and inexpressible, survive and thrive, developing the countless facets and qualities of your personality.

No book could examine all that can possibly occur between the two births. This book will deal with the first birth only tangentially and concentrate on the second birth which is called death. What precedes it, what happens in that second birth and what lies beyond it will be the focus of this book.

Death must be faced. Confrontation with it is the goal of these essays in word and picture. How you face the problem of death and the outcome of that confrontation will determine not only your view of death but even more so your view of life. In the process, much will be said about how to live this life more fully.

Death is a phenomenon which provokes a whole gamut of emotions: fear, anger, resentment, frustration and futility or joy, acceptance, peaceful resignation, hope and faith in some one stronger than death.

Death may seem like a far distant country, but it is one to

which you and I must inevitably journey. This book by its words
and pictures is an attempt to describe that country and provide
a guide to it. The main sections consider the major issues of life,
suffering and death. Reflections on related issues are entitled
"Side Streets" and the reader should view them as invitations
to personal thought and reflection.

Linger on any of the side streets if you like. You will easily
find your way back to the main road when you wish to continue.

If you fear death, this simple travel guide may help you to
overcome some of the causes of that fear. If you are not afraid
of death, you may still discover many things about yourself and
others as you prepare for this journey.

I hope that as you read these pages, pausing to reflect and to
wander down the side streets, you will come to know some of
the interesting points of that strange, but far from imaginary,
country of death. You and I will one day have to pass through
that country to a new life in God's country—our true homeland.

May your journey through these pages bring you to a
deeper knowledge of who you are and where you are going. May
this journey help you to react affirmatively to death as the new
birth and to strengthen your belief in the risen, healing Lord
who calls you to the fullness of life. May these essays and photo-
graphs help prepare you for your final journey home.

Acknowledgment:

I would like to acknowledge with gratitude Sister Mary McGuinness, O.P. and Terry Malone for their invaluable help and editorial expertise, and a group of very loyal typists and assistants, Lynn Ryan, Janet Bladek, Mimi Streleck, Eleanor Parker, Helen Slattery, Theresa Prymuszewski and Sue Lawlor.

CONTENTS

BIRTH TO BIRTH

CHAPTER ONE

THE PUZZLE OF LIFE

QUESTIONING

Have you ever lost someone you loved? How did you react? Did you ever watch another human being die? How did you respond? Did you feel even the slightest hint of Easter joy when death touched you?

Does Easter mean joy and hope in the risen Christ? Does it mean that you and all you love will rise one day with Christ? Or does Easter mean just a day in spring, new clothes and an appearance in church?

Do grey skies and overcast days disturb you? Do they evoke unsettling thoughts about what you are doing with your life, and about what your final end will be? How do you feel when the sunshine pierces the drab and dreary atmosphere of such a day? Can an experience like that be a sign of hope and joy? Can it be a reason to live your life more confidently than ever?

Questions, questions, questions—always questions! Who has the answers?

You do, perhaps, more than you realize.

Some things you know, others you believe on faith. Some are on your lips or in your heart, others are hidden in the depths of your being. You answer many of these questions by your approach to life, for that determines your approach to death.

The complete answer will not be found in this life, but do not underestimate what is already in your mind and heart.

The answer to the problem of life and death will become clearer when you begin looking at your life and yourself as a puzzle. Pieces are missing. But they will be found as you search. For now, why not start with the fact that you are a puzzle?

You and I are puzzles never completely clear to ourselves nor to those we love!

THE PUZZLE

Who can take the measure of another's life?
You and I are puzzles never completely clear
To ourselves nor to those we love.
We build walls to hide behind,
Fearful of full disclosure to anyone—even self.

Most people are content to know a part of us:
Things we've done and plans we've made,
Surface meetings that pose no threat.
But they know us not and often do not care
To make the effort to go beyond the walls.

We let most people see a part of us,
Others a little more of "the real me."
We strive for perfect communion with a few,
Maybe only one or two kindred spirits.
But who truly claims, "I know the real you"?

No matter how we try, the walls surrounding us
Tumble and crumble only so far.
The rubble of our lives still remains
To be picked through, and even then
We remain a mystery only dimly perceived,
Never completely grasped or understood.

God alone knows our hearts and minds,
He, a judge without malice and prejudice,
Renders the verdict which even to us is most just.
His love is a light which pierces our darkness
And frees us from all guilt and shame
For his love puts together the puzzles that we are.

One Who Put the Puzzle Together

Luke's Gospel mentions twice how Mary "pondered all these things in her heart." Mary was trying to put together the pieces of the puzzle of her own life and the life of her extraordinary child.

Why was the savior of the world born in such poor surroundings? Why did so many things happen to him? What was her role in his life? These and many other questions had to be answered before she finally saw the whole picture.

Like Mary, you and I have to put together the puzzle of our lives. Various pieces, big and little, may have to be recognized and integrated into the complete plan of God for us: good and evil, sickness and health, joy and sorrow and, of course, *death*.

Have you tried to fit the pieces of your life-puzzle together? Have you considered the things that happen to you and the ways God reveals himself to you? If you have not, now is the time to begin. Ponder these things in your mind and treasure them in your heart. You will find that the pieces do come together, though not easily. When they do, you will begin to know the why and wherefore of your life. You will be ready to face that special birth, called death.

● *Side Street*

I never thought of Mary as having any difficulties regarding her role in life. And yet I should have known.

Wasn't she upset by the angel's message? Didn't she hesitate and question? Only when she understood her role did she say "yes" to God's plan. She did not say "yes" because she knew every detail of her life and mission. She said "yes" to the God of love who called her in faith to be the mother of his son. God's love would show her how to live her "yes."

Life

The puzzle of each person's life is beautiful because life is beautiful. All the ravages of sickness, age, pain, sinful excess and inhumane treatment which it suffers cannot destroy it. Life is beautiful because it is itself a gift. It is a gift which is beautiful in itself, and becomes more beautiful when one considers who gives it and who receives it.

The Giver

Who gives the gift of life? God does because of love, and his generosity matches his love. We come to understand more about the gift of life as we unwrap it, examine it and use it. Only then do we learn how greatly we are loved. In the same way we grow in love of the giver as we learn more about him through the gift.

Parents are also givers of life, entrusted with the responsibility to conceive, bear and raise new life in love.

God's love is an everlasting love. Parental love is not godly, but it is often a faithful reflection of God's creative love within the limitations of the persons involved.

Children of God's perfect love and their parents' human love are first and foremost children of love. This truth is too often ignored or treated lightly. It deserves better. It provides the key to many of the missing pieces in the puzzle of life.

We may *know* that we are loved by God, parents and others, but that is not enough. We are not disembodied intellects, but thinking, feeling, spiritual, bodily beings.

We need to *feel* love as well as know about it. We must *feel* like children of love. We need to know the joy of a father's warm protective arms engulfing us with tenderness, or the soothing touch of a mother chasing away fear, pain, sadness and feelings of inadequacy. We need not only to be loved, but to be told that we are loved.

● Side Street

The longest journey in the universe is the one from a person's head to his heart especially when the subject is God's love.

Take the journey in stages. Start to talk about God's love and do so often. Slowly but surely your heart will come alive to his love.

The Gift Itself

What is the gift of life? Life is breath and vigor, strength and wholeness. And yet it is more.

It is the joy in God's creation, sorrow at its mistreatment, concern for others. And yet it is more.

Life is Francis, the poor man of Assisi, realizing that worldly goods cannot fulfill his deepest longings. It is loving the birds of the air, the flowers of the field, counting all creatures as universal kin. It is being one with brother sun and sister moon. And yet it is more.

Life is a many-faceted marvel. It has limitations, but often we make them more restrictive than they are. Life is a talent for art and music, for learning and teaching, for giving and receiving, for surprise and sadness, for solitude and friendship. And yet, it is more.

Life is like love because there is always more to it than we realize at any given moment. Life is compassion for another's suffering, joy at another's success. It is an understanding which grasps a situation and knows intuitively what must be done. All this, and yet . . . much more.

Life is an adventure which must be experienced to be grasped, a challenge which must be accepted to be understood, and a time-bound particle of eternity which must be tenderly treasured before it will reveal the secrets which it contains.

● Side Street

To be alive is magic . . . discovered in a brilliant sunburst of feelings called love.

The Recipient

The gift of life creates us as persons. It endows us and empowers us. Such creative life is a treasure to be valued and invested. Perhaps some guidelines for living will help each of us express our own unique giftedness.

Love yourself. Silly, you may say. Of course I love myself. Good, if it is true, but how do you show your love? Think about that. The answer will reveal much to you about the most important person in your life—*you.*

Strive to be the best possible person you can be. You are a gift from a creative God who has delighted in giving you many talents. You have limitations. Admit them and live within them, but only after you have thoroughly probed the boundaries of your abilities. Strive for nothing less than full development of all your talents.

> The highest happiness of man as a thinking being is
> to have probed what is knowable and quietly to revere
> what is unknowable.
>
> —Goethe

You may be talented artistically, literally or mechanically. You may have gifts of perception and compassion, of understanding and humility which will make you a healing presence no matter what profession you enter.

Whatever your abilities are, recognize them. Uncover them if they have lain unused, unnoticed or unrecognized.

Here again love enters the picture. Love can renew you if your growth has been stunted, or your talents have been underdeveloped. Love can make you grow again, and one day bring you to an undreamed-of wholeness.

Love others. Love those who seem lovable and those who do not. God already loves them as he loves all persons. Why not learn to energize your own unique capacity to love by immersing yourself in and reflecting God's perfect love? The uniqueness of your capacity to love is a special gift. Use that gift well. You alone can freely give your love to another. No force or fear can drag it from you. You must decide when to love and whom to love. Try to be as generous in loving others as God is in loving you.

Many people may not seem very lovable, but how lovable would you be if you had not been loved first of all? Could you be the one to convince another of his own value and lovableness? How far are you willing to go in loving others into fuller and happier life?

Hang loose. Enjoy who you are and how you are made. Every day brings its surprises and its opportunities. But thank God, every day does not bring a new crisis. *Don't go about* looking for more crises than you have. Life is meant to be enjoyed. It is meant to re-create us and restore us. Chesterton once wrote: "Joy is the gigantic secret of the Christian." Don't keep your joy so great a secret that even you forget it.

Be open. Have great trust and openness to each day's happenings. Believe that you are called to be and feel heroic, that you are bringing into the world a certain amount of goodness and justice. Be open to what is new and comfortable with what is old.

Do not be afraid to hold up a mirror to yourself. Do so as honestly as possible. It is a great achievement to see yourself for what you are. *Accept* and *love* yourself even with your faults and imperfections, for God knows them better than you and he *loves* you. Be willing to change where change is possible, be accepting of what you cannot change. The important thing is to know the difference.

● *Side Street*

Your life with its many talents and qualities is a gift of love. What does this mean to your family, community and the world? Are there things which you should be doing to make the beauty of life more apparent to yourself and others?

Life View Determines View of Death

"Life is good." "Life is cruel."

"I want to live life fully." "I don't give a damn about it."

"I am a worthwhile person and will be saved." "I am a worthless clod and not worthy of any consideration."

How we wallow in extremes. Balanced judgments and common sense are such valuable—but often missing—pieces in the puzzle of our life. We are told that we are made in the image and likeness of a loving God. But how often does that seem to be merely words?

Believe and *feel* that you are God's beloved child. Strive to make that belief a reality, in fact, the cornerstone on which you build your life here on earth. Keep the image of God as a loving Father and Creator very clear in your own mind and in your own life. Strive to be a creative loving person within the Father's family.

How you perceive yourself and your life has an influence on your perception of death, because both life and death are so closely related.

● Side Street

The subject of death should remind us of how important life is. It should help us to live fully each day and become the best possible person we can be. Why doesn't this always happen?

St. Paul has said that in life and in death we belong to the Lord. Do we truly believe that? Shouldn't such a belief radically change our outlook on what we do with our lives and why we do it?

Life's Peak Experiences

Life has its peaks as well as its plateaus and valleys.

Life has peak experiences when we rise above the routine of daily life and glimpse the wonderful power within us and others, when we glimpse the glorious power of God and his world.

Life's peaks have their purposes. They raise our eyes to the full potential of ourselves and others. But no one can live all of

Life's peak experiences raise our eyes to the full potential of ourselves and others.

life with such intensity. Peaks are followed in life, as in nature, by descents into the valley of the everyday.

Jesus probably had this in mind when he spoke to Peter at the conclusion of the Transfiguration, that extraordinary peak experience for the three chosen apostles. Peter wanted to stay on the mountain top and said: "Master, it is wonderful for us to be here . . ." (Lk 9:33).

Jesus knew better. He told Peter and the others: "Don't pitch your tents here on the mountain top. Go down to the valley and live among your brothers and sisters in God's family. Share the vision that you have received. Tell them that there is more to living than survival, more to being than mere existence and more to becoming than accepting arbitrary limits to your dreams."

Jesus allowed the three apostles to catch a glimpse of his glory so that they would be fortified for his passage to the Lord which was soon to take place in Jerusalem. He wanted them to be ready for his Passion and Death, but also for his Resurrection and Ascension to the glory of the Father. The intense mystical experience of the Transfiguration was not just for the short time it lasted, but for later times as well.

Life's peak experiences are similar. They are to sustain us in whatever trials and difficulties come our way. They are not to be hoarded nor prolonged. We, like the apostles, cannot remain forever on the mountain top. No matter how strong the experience, no matter how intense our joy and satisfaction, there comes a time to move on. And often that will mean going down into the valley of life, and sharing with others the vision that life is beautiful and each part of it is a special gift from the Lord.

To Live or Die

St. Paul said: ". . . I have full confidence that now as well as always, Christ will be exalted through me, whether I live or die. For, to me, 'life' means Christ; hence dying is so much gain. If, on the other hand, I am to go on living in the flesh, that means productive toil for me—and I do not know which to prefer. I am strongly attracted by both: I long to be freed from this life and to be with Christ, for that is the far better thing; yet it is more urgent that I remain alive for your sakes. This fills me with confidence that I will stay with you and persevere with you all, for all your joy and progress in the faith" (Ph 1:20b-25).

● *Side Street*

Death is not to be resisted as the ultimate evil, a fiend in the night waiting to pounce on us. But neither are we to hasten its arrival.

Excesses in eating, drinking, smoking and the pursuit of pleasure can cause us to become flabby physically and often spiritually.

Neither condition is healthy. Neither promotes the fight against damaged life or untimely death.

A Key to Happiness

> *Happy is the one who can rejoice with people of every age and race, of every sex and station. Behold a joyful person.*
>
> *Happy is the one who suffers with others in healing tenderness and quiet presence. Behold a compassionate person.*
>
> *Happy the one who greets life with smiles even though mixed with tears. Behold a courageous person.*
>
> *Happy the one who lives each day completely, and fearlessly lets it pass. Behold a free person.*
>
> *Happy the one who listens, hears and extends a hand to help. Behold an understanding person.*
>
> *Happy the one who gives simply and loves deeply. Behold a sincere person.*
>
> *Happy the one who sings life's alleluias in good times and bad. Behold a grateful person.*
>
> *Happy the one who possesses joy, compassion and courage; freedom, gentleness and understanding; sincerity and gratitude.*

*That person is a gift to self and others, to God and all crea-
tion. That person is truly and fully human, a blessed presence on this earth.*

● *Side Street*

Live with wisdom and grace. Neither quality is automatically attained by living a prescribed number of years. Both are
qualities which have to be learned, developed, and deepened.

Dying Each Day

There is a certain dying that takes place every day. A part of
us dies when we mortify our selfish desires and actions. This is
not the heroic type of mortification often associated with the
saints, but mortification in the ordinary things that make up
our day.

Curbing our tongue, holding back the crushing retort. Helping someone in need. Loving our real neighbor—the people we
live with and rub elbows with each day, the people who irritate
us and whom we irritate.

Dying to selfishness may very well mean being less irritating.
It can be a slow and painful death. Much slower and much more
painful than many illnesses. Dying to selfishness each day in little
ways helps us to cast off all those things that keep us from being
the best person we could be.

Life is an apprenticeship to death, a preparation for our
death. During life, we die to selfishness so that we can be born
anew each day through a deeper love of self, of others and of
God.

Is this not the best preparation for the final death which is
also the final birth to a renewed and perfected self?

Born for Joy or Sorrow

In some parts of the world the father weeps at the birth of
his child and rejoices at its death. Weeps because the baby is

coming into a sinful world and will have to fight against the evil of such a world. Rejoices because his faith assures him that in death the child is taken immediately into the hands of the Father of eternal love.

Such a custom can arouse varied reactions: "barbaric peasant," "simplistic faith," "repulsive approach to human life in our time." Yet there may be some who will whisper: "The first part? Never! But I envy his faith that a loving God waits to receive us at death."

The sinfulness of the world should not make us cry at the birth of a child but rather be a challenge to us as individuals and as members of Christ's people.

The challenge: to raise the child in a faith so strong that his world will be less sinful.

The challenge: to offer that child the wholehearted support of other believers so that he will let Jesus Christ be the light of his life.

Life is a wonderful gift which we receive from God and our parents. But it is how we use that gift and what we put into living that makes it meaningful for us.

● *Side Street*

"When you were born you alone cried and everyone around you was happy. Live your life so that when you die you will be happy and all around you will cry."—*Anonymous*

Wouldn't it be better to live life so well that both you and all around you will be happy because you were here, have died and gone home to the Father?

The Old and the New

Old View

You must suffer in this life for the sake of the next life. This view is often challenged by the question: "What if there is no life after death? What about all your sufferings then?" Believers in immortality can answer that objection, but it is better to accept the new view.

New View

There is joy in this life as well as in the next. Jesus said: "I came that they might have life and have it to the full" (Jn 10:10). God does not want his children to think of this life as a time of unmitigated sorrow and pain. He calls them to live in the freedom and joy of his sons and daughters. In fact, he calls all his children to image him by creatively trying to bring the fullness and joy of life to their world.

Life could always be better, but that does not mean that all of life is simply a trial to be borne, a cross to be shouldered.

What is really at stake here is an earth-bound and limited view of life and death versus God's eternally present view.

God is always and everywhere present to his creation. He sees that there is enough joy and fullness here, and a superabundance of glory after death.

If we could only see things with his eyes—what a difference it would make.

Friendship

Even if life's accomplishments are many and varied, its most significant moments occur in the realm of friendship.

When friendship is true, the kingdom of God is not only within each friend but between them. There is a joy to discovering the sensitivity, the awareness and love which friends share with each other.

True friends have a special capacity to help each other. A person sends out his own signals and vibrations which are clearly understood or mixed with static. A friend listens for each signal and vibration, and tries to hear what is being expressed even though there is static.

Lord, open my eyes to the wonder of my friend.

A friend knows through personal experience how difficult it is to find the right words and so he lovingly waits for the other to express himself. A friend has the time and desire to wait.

One cannot love another as a friend until he has learned to listen in this way. If a friend does not first listen, then he is imposing his own desires instead of being sensitive to the other's needs.

Heidegger has said that "being with develops into listening to." A friend enjoys the fleeting moments of being with, of listening to, and of sharing deeply with the other.

Friendship involves trust, and so a friend willingly allows the other freedom to grow, to become the person he wants to become. There is joy in such growth because to love someone is to help him to grow to maturity.

God has made us in such a way that we can best grow from within only if called forth by someone's love, as Lazarus was called from the tomb by the love of his friend Jesus.

In one sense, friendship is a letting-go which is not unlike the letting-go which death demands. In both friendship and death, *trust* is essential—trust that the friendship will deepen when freedom is guaranteed; trust that death will be the gateway to a new and deeper life.

● *Side Street*

"A faithful friend is a sturdy shelter; he who finds one finds a treasure" (Si 6:14).

No one of us is born a whole person, but each of us can be loved into wholeness by another.

Friendship is two hearts united in a journey toward oneness. It is a renewal of the spirit, a rekindling of love and trust.

PRAYER OF A FRIEND

Lord, increase my capacity to love,
Open my eyes to the wonder of my friend.
Help me to discover the richness and

Beauty burrowed deep within this person.
Let me see, Lord, that the differences between us
Are meant only to enrich and not separate us.

Friendship can exist without you, Jesus.
But not that perfect friendship which we seek.
Lord, be a friend to each of us.
And help us to listen lovingly,
To speak or be silent without fear.
Show us how to deepen our relationship
As we journey together to your home.

Thoughts Turning Inward

A father once told me: "Whenever I used to think about death, I thought about whether my insurance would be enough to provide for my wife and children. Now that I'm older and the children are independent, I think about my death as really being *my* death. I now want to know what death is going to mean to me. What am I going to feel, to do and to think as I die?"

He wondered if he was growing more selfish as the years passed. Of course not! When his loved ones needed him, then he was more concerned about what his death would mean for *them*. Now he had quite naturally begun to think of what his death meant for *him*.

Most productive and responsible people share similar feelings. Such feelings intensify when a person grows older, has less responsibility for others, and begins to feel less productive.

The elderly person who feels needed and productive seems to think far less of death than persons many years younger who lack a compelling reason for living.

That's the answer right there. One needs a strong reason to go on living. The better the reason and the stronger it seems, the more fully will a person live.

So many people are dead long before they die. They desire nothing more from life. They are empty shells waiting to be swept into a watery grave. If only they could catch a glimpse of the amazing freshness of life! There is always so much more to discover, experience, and be.

Let me spend my hours sharing and giving joy to all.

CHAPTER TWO
APPROACHING THE SECOND BIRTH

Aging: A Grace-Filled Process

Lord, teach me to accept age with grace and dignity.

May I carry the treasure of my hard-earned knowledge and
wisdom

With no trace of pride and no illusion of being indispensable.

As I retire from the arena of life's daily triumphs and defeats,

May I understand more of your plan and your perspective
on time and life.

Let me not indulge in self-pity nor console myself with
comments

On young whipper-snappers who aren't even dry behind
the ears.

Rather help me to be useful to those who now must lead
the way.

Let me contribute to them my optimism and prayerful
support.

May I live now serenely content with the present and eager
for the future.

Let me not mourn overmuch the good old days gone by.

May my laying down of daily work be graceful

And as natural as the quiet beauty of evening.

Now in the twilight of my days may I begin to see

How much I have been loved in the past and now am loved
even more.

Your love, as I know it now, is a hint of something better,

Which you have in store for me when this life fades into
the next.

*But while I wait, let me spend my hours sharing and giving
   joy to all,*
*Looking back only to see the pattern of your plan as it
   unfolded.*
*At long last let me understand how you have guided me from
   my mother's womb*
*Through all my days, and how your hand does gently lead
   me now that I am old.*

● *Side Street*

Everything around us is aging.
And we are aging, too.
We have a choice: to let our years slip by or to live each
year as a special gift of grace.

Bruce

Bruce Marsh, a well-known Canadian broadcaster, died of
a heart attack early in 1974 while awaiting a heart transplant. He
was an expert in the field of communications, an active member
of the United Church of Canada and a deeply spiritual man.
Shortly before he died, he spoke of his reactions to the possibility
of death.

"When this thing (the knowledge of the necessity of a heart
transplant) came, it was still a shock. I was struck with the full
impact that at 48 or 49 I was likely to be dead. It isn't supposed
to be a problem if you're a Christian. But this is where the testing
comes in. I found great difficulty in facing it. Then I worked
back from that and now I think that I've faced the worst part—
death.

"You can go back to the Apostles' Creed and find enough to
start with: 'I believe in the resurrection of the body and life everlasting.' If your faith is strong enough, that's all you need. You
can't truly be a Christian if you don't believe in the resurrection
of Christ.

"I would not suggest for a moment that it has been easy.

Many days I spend alone and I have bad days. I spend a lot of time in prayer . . . I spend a fair amount of time reading my Bible . . . You have to have something bigger than Time Magazine or the Reader's Digest.

"I'd like people to know that it really isn't all that difficult. Not everybody has the chance I have had to sit and sort this thing out. I was not pleased with the information that I was likely to die but the inevitability exists for all of us. Your faith, in fact, can make you strong" (*The Canadian Register*, Toronto—May 4, 1974).

● *Side Street*

How many of us can count on having as much time to prepare for death as Bruce had? Do his reflections on death and dying offer us any food for thought?

Flat on Your Back

Have you ever heard the expression, "When you're flat on your back there's only one way to look and that's up." At such a time, you can raise your heart, eyes and mind to God and to spiritual realities. You can look up and see all these things, or nothing at all—depending on your frame of mind.

How good it is at those moments to see a kind, considerate human being ministering to you, to see the soft caressing smile of a loved one. The healing power of love can be seen in the smallest act of kindness. Love should be mixed with every medication, every word of advice, and every visit.

People who are loving and concerned, tender and yet firm, compassionate and caring help make God's presence real. Pray that such people will be near you if you're ever flat on your back.

● *Side Street*

A jetty thrusts out into the Atlantic from the Jersey shoreline. Perched upon it, seemingly driven into its very foundations,

An invitation to believe in the Christ of the Cross.

stands a series of crosses. One is quite large, the other five or six are smaller.

Why were they put there? I do not know.

Could they be the remains of a game once played and now forgotten?

A sign of commitment too deep for mere words?

A call for all to know Jesus and his cross?

I find in those crosses an invitation to believe in the Christ of the cross who answers all our questions regarding suffering and death in the only convincing way—by his own life, death and resurrection.

Assisi: A Different Way of Caring for the Sick

The wife of an Anglican clergyman, while visiting Assisi, Italy, was hit by a car. At the local hospital a doctor examined her and prescribed the treatment. The nurse took care of the medicine, but the family, in this case, her husband, was supposed to provide for all her other needs. Feeding and bathing the patient, keeping her comfortable and visiting her were a full time job for the clergyman.

In his view the hospital was primitive in its accommodations. But as the days passed he saw the value of involving the family in the total care of the patient. He soon realized that when he was not able to be with his wife, the families of the other patients made sure that she never wanted for anything.

Their family spirit was so strong that they eagerly shared it with this very proper English woman. They cared for her and fed her from their own limited resources. They also showed many signs of kindness to the husband, as he lived through those anxious days.

Modern hospitals offer many more conveniences than the hospital in Assisi, but the Anglican clergyman was quite convinced that his wife recovered more quickly because of the truly loving care she received from himself and her "adopted families" while at the hospital in Assisi.

Three Valiant Women

Dr. Elizabeth Kubler-Ross treats of death and dying at great length in her book by that title and in her many lectures and articles. She has interviewed hundreds of dying persons and identified five stages which a terminally ill person usually experiences. She demands that the dying patient be treated as a *person* and be given warm, loving support and companionship through the various stages of dying.

Dr. Cecily Saunders built St. Christopher's Hospice in London to provide a community of concern, companionship and love for the terminally ill. Many taboos about death, especially the one which forbids expressing one's feelings about it, are destroyed at St. Christopher's Hospice. This is done, not so much by any "fiat" of the director, as by the very atmosphere of the community.

There are several groups at the hospice: elderly people in good health have a wing of their own; terminally ill patients are not "housed" but given a home in their own wards and rooms; children of the staff delight the older generation as they attend the nursery school provided by the hospice. Everyone is helped to feel a part of the total community. This has been remarkably successful in providing a peaceful setting for people. At times this loving home-like atmosphere has resulted in the remission of an illness and sometimes in what certainly looks like a cure.

Mother Teresa of Calcutta and her Missionaries of Charity dedicate themselves to caring for the dying destitute. She and her followers feel called by God to do something beautiful for the least of his creatures. They care for the poorest of the poor with the simplest of materials but with the greatest of love.

"We have it in our power to be in heaven with God right now—to be happy with him at this very moment. But being happy with him now means:

    loving as he loves,
    helping as he helps,
    giving as he gives,

serving as he serves,
rescuing as he rescues,
being with him 24 hours,
touching him in his distressing disguise."

—Mother Teresa of Calcutta

Doctors Kubler-Ross and *Saunders* and *Mother Teresa of Calcutta* command our admiration, attention and respect. All three are professionals, competent in several areas, and highly sensitive. They have seized the opportunity offered them, but even more so, have been seized by the unexpected challenge and opportunity that came their way. They have done the immensely difficult task: helping the terminally ill to combat the fear of death and of dying alone.

But what about us? What can we do? Follow our own lights, live our own lives, *but* with an increased awareness of the needs of the sick and the dying.

Some elements of the lives of these three valiant women can be incorporated into our own lives. Who of us does not have an elderly relative or friend? Aren't there nursing homes or hospitals in our neighborhood? A visit to such places will reveal lonely people hungering for nothing more than just a few moments of our time and presence.

● *Side Street*

A seriously ill or dying person is just that—*a person* with rights, dignity, needs, and desires, *who happens to be seriously ill or dying.*

Talking with the Dying

When Dr. Kubler-Ross began her investigations into the attitudes and thoughts of dying people, she was surprised at many things. First of all, few people on the medical or nursing staff of the hospital would admit that anyone was dying unless the patient was actually expiring.

When she was finally able to talk with terminally ill people and discuss their feelings with them, she discovered how much they wanted to talk. Finally the wall of silence was breached and the dying were able to discuss the question which haunted their minds. Previously the people who had been most willing to listen to the patients' feelings and fears were the cleaning staff, who were not embarrassed by such confidence. They also found the time to do many small things which had great significance for the patient.

Very few people want to play games with the doctor, the nurses or their families. And yet so often they are forced to make believe that they do not know what is going on in their bodies. They must play the game of "You'll get well" when they know they will never recover. Such patients told Dr. Kubler-Ross that they would much prefer to use their energies in living fully until they died rather than playing an almost grotesque game of charades.

To Tell or Not to Tell

One of the most difficult decisions to make is whether or not to tell a terminally ill person that he is dying. Will the person give up all hope and be almost destroyed by such news? Or will he deeply appreciate the confidence that has been shown in him and the time to put his affairs in order?

There is no easy answer to this question. I have a very strong feeling that many people know before they are told. We humans have a great capacity to delude ourselves, but, an equally great capacity to finally face the truth. It is very difficult for someone in our day to undergo extensive tests and treatment without some suspicion of a serious illness.

The family, the doctor, the hospital staff, and the clergy, in their talks and visits with the dying patient, can get some idea of how the patient feels and what he suspects. One barrier that prevents the patient's feelings and suspicions from getting through is the fear that the family, doctor and clergymen themselves have of death. Sometimes they are determined to fight death to the very last ounce of the patient's resources, while the patient is far more ready to accept. Dr. Kubler-Ross has shown how desperately terminally ill patients want to dispense with playing games and to talk about the gut issues of life and death. It is not one person's responsibility to decide whether to tell or not. The doctor, the family, and the clergy should consult with one another and carefully and prayerfully make the decision. It is the doctor's responsibility to do the actual telling but the family and the clergy should be there to support the person once he has received the news.

The conclusion to this question is that there is no general rule except to try to be on the same wave length as the patient, to keep one's own fears in the background, and to give the greatest consideration and respect to the patient.

The Stages of Dying

Dr. Kubler-Ross in her research has identified five stages that most terminally ill people experience. She also identified a related five stages that the families of dying people experience.

The terminally ill person may experience:

1. Denial: "It couldn't happen to me."
2. Anger: "Why me?"
3. Bargaining: "Just give me another week (month, year) and I'll be ready (go to church or synagogue, give my body to science, etc.").
4. Depression: "No one cares or understands. I'm all alone."
5. Acceptance: "I know it's time and I'm ready to go." This is not bitter resignation to an inevitable fact, but a weariness with fighting any more and turning inward to prepare for death.

● Side Street

When visiting a terminally ill person, try to realize what

stage he may be experiencing. You may provide him with an outlet for many pent up emotions if you can empathize with him and not let his anger or depression throw you off balance.

Fear and the Dying

Fear can be a constant companion of those who are sick or dying. Fear has many disguises—the fear of the unknown, the fear of being alone and the fear of pain which intensifies our sufferings.

We humans are beset by so many fears, and they seem to surface most forcefully when we are seriously ill or suspect that we are dying.

It is important to realize that fear will be there at such times and to understand why it is there and what, if anything, can be done about it.

No matter how old we are, part of us is still a child. A child's fear feeds on the minor discomforts and inconveniences of normal patient care. A child's fear must be seen for what it is and efforts made to ease it. The patient experiencing such fear must be soothed and reassured as we would do with any worried and frightened child.

An adult fear arises when the ultimate questions are faced. What is death? What will it mean for me and for my loved ones? What comes after death? Reading about such things now, reflecting upon them and confronting their implications will modify and lessen that type of fear.

No thing will remove our fears completely. *Some One* might. And to many of us, that someone is our loving God and Father who is stronger than fear, stronger than death itself.

● Side Street

Fear has been compared to another person living within us who will always have the upper hand unless we tear away his mask of anonymity.

Fear faced in faith is fear weakened.
Fear faced with Jesus is fear conquered.

Suffering in Union with Jesus

Your cross, my Lord, has now been offered me.
I accept, but we both know how weak I am—
I am so frightened by the burden and the pain.
I accept the cross, my Lord, because it is yours
And you will not let me carry it alone.
Your strong shoulders will strengthen my weakened frame.

You are the Lord of life, my brother, my savior, my constant
companion.
You will heal me of that fear which only intensifies my pain.
You can and would heal me of my illness if I but ask you.
I do not ask; for I hear your call to the cross
And know that with you and in you I am now called
To help save our world, more desperately in need of health
than I.

My prayer, my brother, is a simple one.
Be with me and in me during all the days to come.
Give me more joy than pain to bear.
More happiness than sadness, more truth than doubt.
More hope than desolation, more vitality than boredom.
Finally, my brother, may my soul and spirit be vibrant with
health.

I accept the cross of my illness, but in your love
I know that you will not allow that cross to come alone.
These are the conditions of my covenant with you, Lord.
For what I truly want is what you, too, seek.
I want more life than death, a life beyond all death.
A life which does not die, a life with you, my Lord.

I accept the cross, my Lord, because it is yours, and you will not let me carry it alone.

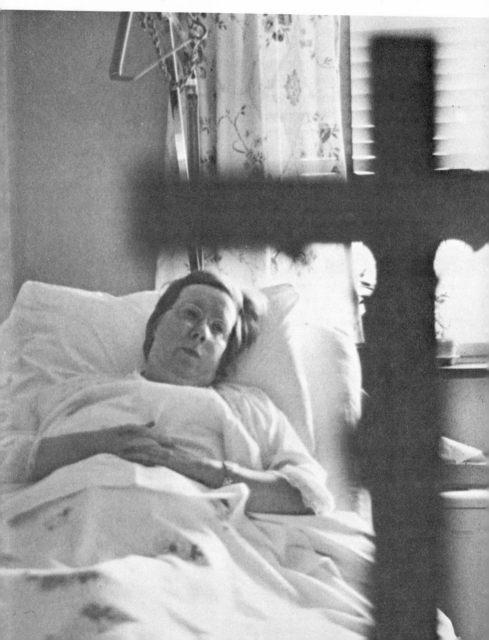

Never Alone

Jesus said, "Behold I am with you always, even to the end of time." We usually take "always" to refer to time and duration. We could broaden its application by interpreting "always" to mean "in all ways." "I am with you at all times and in all the ways you will need me to be with you."

"You, Lord, are my shepherd and my constant companion, my pace-setter and my pace-maker, my heart-beat and my delight. Now that I am sick I need to know that all these titles are not merely words, but express how close you are and how much you mean to me.

"Whenever I feel alone, rejected or afraid, don't let me become so absorbed in myself and my problems that I forget to turn to you. Help me to understand that you are always with me and will never fail to answer my call for help.

"At certain times I may begin to doubt your love or to feel that you take too long in answering my call. At those moments please send me a sign of your love in someone or something."

Praying with the Sick and the Dying

Pray lovingly with the sick or dying person, in words, psalms, snatches of favorite hymns or meaningful silences.

Pray with your body—holding hands and even embracing.

Pray with your heart and soul, and pray in the Spirit always.

Pray for all that God our Father wants to give that person at this special moment.

Pray prudently, attentive to the pain and fear of the dying. Your silence or your hand in theirs may say more than the most eloquently spoken prayer.

Prayer is not a plunge into the morass of self-pity. It is not the recitation of words well-said but little-meant, like children in a play mouthing lines with little sense of their meaning.

Prayer is turning from self to God and entering into communion with him in every way we can. Prayer is recognizing how much we need God and responding to the fact that he is present to us at all times.

St. James put it very well. He urged his people to pray when suffering hardship, but when they were sick, he knew that they might need the prayerful support of other believers. Therefore he advised the sick person to "ask for the presbyters of the church. They in turn are to pray over him, anointing him with oil in the Name (of the Lord.) This prayer uttered in faith will reclaim the one who is ill, and the Lord will restore him to health. If he has committed any sins, forgiveness will be his. Hence, declare your sins to one another, and pray for one another, that you may find healing" (Jm 5:14-16).

Prayer is effective in healing if it is "uttered in faith." Such prayer proceeds from faith and is pursued in faith. The faith on which healing prayer rests is an expectant faith—a faith that firmly expects the Lord to restore the sick person to health and forgive his sins.

"The fervent petition of a holy man (or woman) is powerful indeed" (Jm 5:16). That power springs from the close relationship a holy person has with God, a relationship which is nourished by and expressed in prayer of every type.

● *Side Street*

Mary, the mother of Jesus, was a holy woman and her prayer was and is powerful indeed. Through the waters of Lourdes she makes us aware of the healing power of God which conquers sin, suffering and even death. Miracles really are worked at Lourdes as they are at other shrines. For some they are physical miracles, for others spiritual.

Mary does not do it alone. She has power to heal only because of who she is: a woman acquainted with hard work, pain and suffering, even as she knew the joy and happiness of serving her God. Because she suffered, she knows how to comfort us in our suffering. Her healing touch is that of a loving mother who knows when and how her children need her.

The Anointing of the Sick—I

An elderly woman who had been quite ill woke up one night to find her hospital room filled with people. Suddenly, she realized that she was receiving the sacrament of the Anointing of the Sick. Noticing her confusion, a nurse whispered gently in her ear that she was going to be all right.

Calmed by the nurse's words but more by her manner, the patient began to listen more carefully to the prayers of the anointing. She joined her family as they answered the prayers.

The loving support of so many people strengthened her. The fear that had assaulted her in the first moments of consciousness disappeared as she realized how loved she was by God, her family and her Church. She recovered from her illness more fully aware of the healing love of God at work in his Church and especially in the sacrament of the Anointing of the Sick.

● *Side Street*

How would you feel if you awoke tonight and found yourself in similar circumstances?

The Anointing of the Sick—II

I remember vividly the anointing of an elderly college professor. The cancer which he had fought so determinedly finally began to win the battle. Returning from the hospital after medical science had done all that it could, he was cared for with loving warmth and kindness by some of his former students.

As his sufferings drew to a close he was surrounded by many of the students whom he had taught, befriended and loved over the years. When he died he went to God consoled by their prayers, especially the Rosary which he revered so much.

Alongside that scene there is another which I remember well. It is of the last time he was anointed. In a reaffirmation of their humanity, the priest who was administering the sacrament knelt by the bed and took the hand of the dying man. Together they prayed with great fervor.

Such warm touches make the sacrament more meaningful. These beautiful sacramental signs and ceremonies are meant to express what Jesus himself did. He always acted with loving compassion and tender awareness of his kinship with the sick.

To share such experiences with the dying—to share their fear and their pain and their love—is to face one of life's most challenging moments. To do so with tender compassion and love adds glory to our common humanity and destiny.

● *Side Street*

A man had cancer of the esophagus and could eat only the blandest of foods. His daughter spent many hours looking for foods which could appeal to him. She wanted his last year to be a time of happiness in many ways but especially at the lovingly prepared meals she and her mother shared with him. A nurse, who was an extraordinary minister of the Eucharist, brought him communion while his daughter was visiting. He only managed to swallow a small particle of the host, so the nurse asked the daughter if she would like to receive the remainder. She was overjoyed to be able to share this special meal with her father.

When she speaks of this experience, her face glows with a quiet beauty. For her, that Eucharist was the best of all the meals she and her father had so lovingly shared.

Viaticum: The Sacrament of the Dying

"The sacrament of the dying" is a phrase most often used for the Anointing of the Sick. The actual sacrament of the dying is the Eucharist, under the special title of "Viaticum." It is a Latin word which means "on the way with you" or "provisions for a journey."

I like to think of Viaticum as having two interpretations. The Lord coming in a special way and saying: "Do not be afraid. I am with you on the journey home."

The other interpretation has the person say to Jesus, "I am making this journey with you in whom is all my hope. You have died and risen from the dead. Death no longer has dominion over you. I am safe with you." Both interpretations are extraordinarily comforting.

● *Side Street*

The Eucharist: A Pledge of Eternal Life

A dying woman could retain no solid food except the Eucharist during the last three weeks of her illness. Each day she waited eagerly for the "food of life." She found in the Eucharist the special nourishment she needed to live her life fully to the very end. Did she also see in the Eucharist "the pledge of eternal glory," an effect of this sacrament that is too often forgotten?

Shirley

Shirley, a very young woman of 40, had just been told she had cancer. Soon after, as Lent began, she received ashes on her forehead to signify her willingness to do penance, and heard the words, "Repent and believe the good news."

She could very well have asked, "Believe what good news?" That she had to face long months of painful treatments? That there was only a slight possibility of a remission, little chance for a cure and most likely death?

The good news that she believed was not about her sickness but about herself. God loved her. She believed that God the Father was saying, "You are my beloved child and my love will support you no matter what you have to endure during your sickness."

God the Son, but also her Brother-Savior, comforted her with the words, "You are my beloved sister and I will be with you as you travel the path of sickness to the end." God the Holy Spirit whispered gently, "You are my temple, my chosen vessel. I will be with you always. Together we will sanctify this time of your life."

Christmas found her weak but filled with its true spirit. She

Francis was willing to let go of many things to gain the true freedom and happiness for which God had made him.

personally made and distributed Christmas decorations for the door of each patient's room. Each year since her death, the Christmas decorations are hung on the doors. What vibrant love for others they represent!

Shirley lives today in the hearts and minds of many of her friends and students. Some pray to her for guidance. Her example still inspires them to be a gift of love to others as she was to them.

Shirley lives today in the fullness of life with God. She loved her life and lived it fully while on earth, but she was willing to let go of it in order to complete the journey from birth to birth. She lives now forever in joy, peace and love.

Our Brother Who Lived Freely

St. Francis of Assisi loved life like few individuals ever did. But he knew what he wanted and it was something more than the life of a wealthy merchant's son. He was willing to let go of many things to gain the true freedom and happiness for which God had made him.

Declaration of Independence

"I want to be happy, I want to live like the birds in the sky. I want to experience the freedom and purity they experience. The rest is no use to me. No use. Believe me. If the purpose of life is this loveless toil we fill our days with, then it's not for me. There must be something better. There *has* to be.

"Man is a spirit. He has a soul. And that—that is what I want to recapture. My soul. I want to live in the fields, stride over hills, climb trees, swim rivers. I want to feel the firm grasp of the earth beneath my feet without shoes, without possessions, without those shadows we call our servants.

"I want to be a beggar. Yes, yes, a beggar. Christ was a beggar and his holy apostles were beggars. I want to be as free as they are."

— St. Francis of Assisi (from the film
Brother Sun, Sister Moon)

To Live and Die in Peace

Often it is said that a person took a breath, sighed and died. How peaceful!

Could this not be reassuring to us who fear death so very much? The sigh may be a sign of completion and contentment as the passageway to another life is opening.

Jesus on the cross said:

> "Father, into your hands I commend my spirit"
> (Lk 23:46).

The sigh of the dying person may very well be a way of saying:

> "Into your hands, O Lord, I bring myself and all that I am. It is finished. I fight no more. Now I place all my trust in your loving care."

We might be more consoled if angels came to take our loved one home in literal fulfillment of the words of the ancient Christian funeral hymn: "May the angels take you into paradise . . ." But do we really need such proof of God's love? Has he not proved his love in the life, death and resurrection of his Son, our brother Jesus?

A child frequently falls asleep protesting that he is not tired. He vainly fights to stay awake.

A sleepy person needs to sleep; a dying person needs to die. Death can be as natural as sleep. There comes a time when it is unreasonable as well as useless to resist either sleep or death.

But how can we know when to fight for life and when to prepare ourselves to be born again? Such discernment is not easy to attain but some things should be considered. Age, weakness, responsibilities to others, and one's own personal spiritual, emotional and psychological needs must be weighed when deciding whether or not to continue the fight.

How can any of us live with the idea of giving up the fight

and preparing to die? By refusing to become wholly preoccupied with it and choosing instead to integrate the fear, pain and weakness into the total mystery of life. Living full and integrated lives in the face of death is the ideal.

● *Side Street*

> *"At all times we carry in our mortal bodies the death of Jesus, so that his life also may be seen in our bodies"*
>
> (2 Cor 4:10)

Fr. Martin and I stood at the side of the bed of Sr. Loretta Ann, O.P., who was near death from bone cancer. We gave her our blessing. We came to give and we also received. A powerful, sacred presence surrounded the three of us. Our crucified Lord seemed to be tangibly present to his pain-filled sister. In some way, we were touched and healed by the powerful life that reigned in this dying woman. It was a life so vibrant it all but overshadowed the physical death that was so near."

—Father Ken. St. Amand.

How and When to Die

Some people seem to die too soon, others die too late; few seem to die at the right time.

You probably want to die at the right time, don't you? But what is the right time? Do you want the burden of making that judgment? Be assured that it is an awesome burden.

How would you like to die? Suddenly with no long months of illness? Slowly, even painfully, but with time to prepare?

It isn't easy to decide, is it? And when and if you do decide, will you always feel the same? You don't know how you'll feel when you're older or when death becomes more imminent.

The right time to die may never be clear beforehand. The right way to die is quite clear—lovingly.

● *Side Street*

A minister who was told that he was dying of leukemia responded:

"I knew I had to die of something and leukemia is as good as anything. Besides I have been heading in that direction all my life."

When he was dying on the cross Jesus said to the Father: "Into your hands, O Lord, I commend my spirit." It is a beautiful phrase which should grace our lips often. Whenever danger threatens and makes me realize more intently how frail I am, I pray those words.

Prayer of Abandonment

FATHER:

I abandon myself into your hands;
Do with me what you will.
Whatever you may do, I thank you:
I am ready for all, I accept all.
Let only your will be done in me,
And in all your creatures—
I wish no more than this, O Lord.

Into your hands I commend my soul;
I offer it to you with all the love of my heart,
For I love you, Lord,
And so need to give myself,
To surrender myself into your hands,
Without reserve,
And with boundless confidence,

For you are my Father.

—Brother Charles of Jesus

Folk Wisdom

Folk wisdom tells us: "If a thing is worth doing, it's worth doing well."

Following this we might say: "You are most assuredly going to die, so die well. Die like a person of faith. When you know that death is coming, face it bravely. Let the best of you show through."

But an intellectual might say: "If a thing is worth doing, then it's worth doing badly." This second, more startling comment contains some truth. If a thing is worth doing, then it is worth doing no matter how it's done. Even if it's done badly, it is still worth doing.

Following the second axiom, we might offer this advice: "If you can die only fearfully and with just a glimmer of hope, it's worth doing. Hold on to that hope even if you are afraid and feel so alone. All is not lost as long as you have that hope."

You must die, but you need not die badly. You might even surprise yourself by dying rather well. And that would inspire others to die well also.

● *Side Street*

"Nothing would be done at all if a man waited until he could do something so well that no one could find fault with it!"
—John Henry Cardinal Newman

Hope for the Living and the Dying

To live without hope is sad, but to die without hope is indeed a tragedy. Both the living and the dying must have hope.

Hope for the living is hope for recovery from illness. It is hope that there will be time to love and care for family and friends, and to complete the many tasks still undone. It is hope that life will be lived more fully than before.

The dying also have hope but, in many ways, it is more basic than that of the living.

The hope of the dying person is that the pain will not be too intense, and that he will not die lonely, isolated and abandoned. It is the hope that he will be allowed to die with dignity as a person and as a Christian. It is the hope that he will be treated as one who is, before all else, a person who happens to be dying. Above all, it is hope in a God who will lovingly lead his child home.

Christians can rely on God's promise of having Jesus Christ as their firm anchor of hope.

"God, wishing to give the heirs of his promise even clearer evidence that his purpose would not change, guaranteed it by oath, so that . . . we who have taken refuge in him might be strongly encouraged to seize the hope which is placed before us. Like a sure and firm anchor, that hope extends beyond the veil through which Jesus, our forerunner, has entered on our behalf" (Heb 6:17-20).

A Parable

Once upon a time, twin boys were conceived in the same womb. Seconds, minutes, hours passed as the two dormant lives developed. The spark of life glowed until it fanned fire with the formation of their embryonic brains. With their simple brains came feeling, and with feeling, perception; a perception of surroundings, of each other, of self.

When they perceived the life of each other and their own life, they knew that life was good, and they laughed and rejoiced: the one saying, "Lucky are we to have been conceived, and to have this world," and the other chiming, "Blessed be the Mother who gave us this life and each other."

Each budded and grew arms and fingers, lean legs and stubby toes. They stretched their lungs, churned and turned in their new-found world. They explored their world, and in it found the life cord which gave them life from the precious Mother's blood. So they sang, "How great is the love of the

Mother that she shares all she has with us!" And they were pleased and satisfied with their lot.

Weeks passed into months, and with the advent of each new month, they noticed a change in each other and each began to see change in himself. "We are changing," said the one. "What can it mean?"

"It means," replied the other, "that we are drawing near to birth."

An unsettling chill crept over the two, and they both feared, for they knew that birth meant leaving all their world behind.

Said the one, "Were it up to me, I would live here forever."

"We must be born," said the other. "It has happened to all others who were here." For indeed there was evidence of life there before, as the Mother had borne others.

"But mightn't there be a life after birth?"

"How can there be life after birth?" cried the one. "Do we not shed our life cord and also the blood tissues? And have you ever talked to one that has been born? Has anyone ever re-entered the womb after birth?"

"No!" He fell into despair, and in his despair he moaned, "If the purpose of conception and all our growth is that it be ended in birth, then truly our life is absurd."

Resigned to despair, the one stabbed the darkness with his unseeing eyes and as he clutched his precious life cord to his chest said, "If this is so, and life is absurd, then there really can be no Mother."

"But there is a Mother," protested the other. "Who else gave us nourishment and our world?"

"We get our own nourishment, and our world has always been here. And if there is a Mother, where is she? Have you ever seen her? Does she ever talk to you? No! We invented the Mother because it satisfied a need in us. It made us feel secure and happy."

Thus while one raved and despaired, the other resigned himself to birth, and placed his trust in the hands of the Mother.

Hours ached into days, and days fell into weeks. And it came time. Both knew their birth was at hand, and both feared what they did not know. As the one was the first to be conceived, so he was the first to be born, the other following after.

They cried as they were born into the light. And coughed out fluid and gasped the dry air. And when they were sure they had been born, they opened their eyes, seeing for the first time, and found themselves cradled in the warm love of the Mother! They lay open-mouthed, awe-struck before that beauty and truth they could not hoped to have known.

(Published in *Agape*, September, 1975, vol. 4, no. 9, page 19)

Love Conquers All

Love is strong enough to conquer death and dying, taking the fear from those frightening moments. Yet not every love is so strong even though it is sometimes heralded as a tough and everlasting thing, as a quality that will last forever once it has been pledged.

Love itself can die. It can be starved ever so slowly but steadily to death by neglect and misuse.

Love is fragile and tender. It needs much care if it is to grow strong and resilient. As an acorn needs good soil and enough sunshine and rain to become that fabled mighty oak, so love needs many things to grow strong enough to conquer death.

When we love another we enrich the other person by giving what is most alive in us, our joy and sadness, our interest and concern, our understanding and knowledge. As we love, we give the best we have, but also allow the other person to give us what is most alive in him. Then together we rejoice in what our mutual loving has brought to life.

A Christian—one who follows Christ—is by definition a person who loves. "See how these Christians love one another." A Christian worthy of the name shares the riches of the Christian mystery—the faith, hope and love which animate him, as well as the deep sense of union with Jesus that drives him on.

The Christian's joy in loving springs from the conviction that he is striving to give life. His joy is not diminished by the realization that this can only happen if he is willing to die to self like the grain of wheat in the Gospel story. A love like that which is anchored in Christ is strong enough for life, for death and forever.

How Have We Loved?

Saint John of the Cross tells us that in the evening of our lives we shall be examined on how we have loved. How have we valued love? Have we given and received it in wonder and reverence? Have we spent it? Hoarded it?

Love is a God-like gift; for God is love and the source of all our love. In loving, the divine spark deep within us springs into flame. Love is a fire which we need if we are to live and to die well. It is a fire which grows stronger only when we give it to another and allow the other to give it in return.

● *Side Street*

"True love
   is delicate and kind,
   full of gentle
   perception and understanding,
   full of beauty and grace,
   full of unutterable
     JOY."
     —Dorothy Day

"Some day after mastering
   the winds, the waves, the tides and gravity,
we shall harness for God
   the energies of
     LOVE.

And then for the second time
   in the history of the world

man will have discovered
        FIRE."
                —Teilhard de Chardin

"Real love is full of living and dying:
    It takes the best that a person is
because it takes all that a person is."
            —Eugene Kennedy, M.M.

CHAPTER THREE

DEATH AND BIRTH

Death Comes but Not Alone

As a leaf separated from the tree,
As a drop of water drawn into the ocean,
As a speck of sand blown about by the wind,
As a child lost in a crowd,
As a man wandering at night in a deserted cemetery,
As lonely and insignificant as these
Come I to the subject of death.

I seem so small and death looms so large,
One thought only gives me hope:
Jesus carved a path through that alien land
He only is the way, the truth and the life,
Jesus is the way for me
Leading to that second birth
Where life unending and complete begins.

Jesus is the truth which beckons me
To leave every doubt and fear I have
And place all my trust in him.
Jesus is the life that lives forevermore,
And in Him I find the life
I dared not dream could ever be mine.
Jesus is my greatest comfort and my greatest challenge
As I journey home.

Let us find the Lord's footprints in all of life's experiences and follow them.

Footprints in the Sands

Footprints in the sands of life. Sometimes clear, inviting, almost compelling, they seem to cry out: "Come, follow me. Do not be afraid. I have gone before you."

At other times vague, confusing, almost frightening, "Flee!" they seem to hiss.

The footprints seem contradictory, the path unclear. Which way shall we go?

Death has, we know, walked this way before. But so has Christ.

Jesus Christ is the answer; for he is
> *"the way, and the truth and the life"*
> (Jn 14:5).

Let us find his footprints in all of life's experiences and follow them. He alone can safely lead us home.

On the way we need not fear the darkness because Jesus tells us:

> *"I am the light of the world.*
> *No follower of mine shall ever*
> *walk in darkness;*
> *No, he shall possess the light of life"*
> (Jn 8:12).

Death Itself Comes

No person has truly died and then returned to tell us about it. Jesus died and rose, but did not teach us about the many things which fascinate us regarding death. After the resurrection, he spent his time with the apostles reassuring them that he was truly risen and alive. He told them "about the kingdom of God" (Ac 1:3) and prepared them to be his messengers.

Are we completely ignorant about death? No, but neither do we have answers to all our questions.

3

Beauty of Death

Death as life has a beauty of its own, though it is not always readily apparent. It is hidden by layers of fear, frustration and failure to understand its purpose.

The beauty of death rests mainly on its promise of quiet bliss and exhilarating activity, of the joy of new life and reunion with loved ones, and of perpetual absorption in the wonder of God's love.

Some recognize death's beauty, others are revolted by such a thought. Still others wonder why all the fuss. Death is death and that's it. Why confuse the matter by further speculation.

A married couple once agreed that if one of them died the other would grieve only so long and then use the insurance money to travel. The husband remarked a little later, "When one of us dies, *I'll* go to Paris."

How simple it is to admit that others are going to die. But never me. Only *you* die, never *me!*

Death is too complex to be put on the back burner. It must be faced and understood.

● *Side Street*

The very cells by which our bodies function are constantly changing. In fact the growing cells of our bodies are completely replaced approximately every seven years. Consequently, there should be no surprise that in the second birth—the birth that we call death—our physical make-up is changed quite drastically.

Teilhard de Chardin, while serving in the trenches during World War I, was asked if he had any fear of death. No, he replied, because he believed that when he died, he would just change his state of being. That's not a bad description of what happens at death. I change, but *I* still am.

Death is inevitable. It is not the end of all, but just one more change. Admittedly a very important one.

Death—No Stranger

Some people today are obsessed with death, but try to sweep it under the rug—an approach comparable to the Victorian attitude toward sex. The "ignore it" approach to death is a surface reaction covering deep anxiety. This suppressed anxiety surfaces in many ways.

For some, even the most minor illness is viewed as terminal. Cancer is almost the first thought that pops into their minds when they have anything more than a common cold.

Some seek eternal youthfulness or its appearance.

Others strive to assert their masculinity or femininity in a variety of ways. They must have the biggest and best of everything—house, car, clothing, business, boat vacation, expense account and so on.

Ignored or suppressed death means a stranger of our own making—but only for a time. Death visits all. How we plan to receive it is the important question.

Defects of Death: Blind and Deaf

Death is both blind and deaf. *Blind:* it does not look to see if its victim is young or old, healthy or weak, productive or not, man or woman, adult or child. *Deaf:* it does not hear our cries for just a little more time to live, to straighten out our affairs, to do all of the tomorrow things our todays overlooked.

Many times it seems a pity that a person with so much to offer the world has to die before the prime of life. Death has much to say about timing—but I don't believe it has the final word. Love is stronger than death and love will have the final word. As Albert Camus put it, "In the midst of Winter, I finally learned that there was in me an invincible Summer."

Death is no weakling. This view just puts death in its place—a strong *second* to love.

Graced Moments

We who believe in the power of love, who believe that our God is love, have a secret weapon against the destructive forces of death. We have a vision of life and death which helps us face both with open arms and eyes.

Certain times in life are graced moments in which God touches us in the deepest parts of our being. Death, the end of life and the birth to another life, can be such a moment if we let it be. In that graced moment, our God, who is neither deaf nor blind, comes in love to take us home.

We begin to die as soon as we are born. Do we not also begin to live as soon as we die? Birth is death (to life in the womb), death is a birth (to life everlasting).

In the first birth we cut the cord that has bound us to our mother. But we do not destroy the relationship; we begin to live it in a new way.

In the birth called death we cut the cord that has bound us to this earth, but we do not destroy all relationship with the earth or its people. We experience a new dimension in that relationship.

● Side Street

Naked I came forth from my mother's womb, and naked shall I be born again from mother earth's womb (Paraphrase of Jb 1:21).

Will they put my job with me in my coffin? My home? My empire whether big or small?

No false god but self fits into a coffin and in death the idol self neither looks nor smells divine.

Problem and Mystery

When you think about death, do you see it as a problem to be solved or as a mystery to be experienced?

A problem is something you can put your hands on, measure,

diagram. There is a good chance that you can solve it, either alone or with help.

A mystery is far different. It eludes attempts to grasp and control it. A mystery yields only when you plunge into it. Even then you may discover only a partial solution.

Death is a problem. When, where and why it happens are just some aspects of the problem.

Death is also a mystery. It is too vast to be encompassed in words or pictures. Naming the shafts of understanding which pierce the darkness of the mystery is like naming a whirlwind, and yet, it must be attempted.

Try three as beginners: Faith, Hope and Love. By these three the power of God pierces the mystery of death.

Flashes of comprehension are possible, but the complete answer comes only by full participation. We—you and I—must die to know the answer.

● *Side Street*

A student once tried to paint death. She covered the canvas with dark colors, but at the edge near the top right-hand corner had a shaft of light beginning to shine through. For her death was not the end but only the doorway to resurrection.

"Death is not darkness. It is turning down the lamp when dawn has broken."—Tagore.

Japanese Folk Tale

There was a boy on a small island which was threatened by tidal waves and volcanic eruptions. He was afraid of dying and he wanted to know if grown-ups felt the same. So he asked a man if he was also afraid to die.

The man, who vividly remembered his own fears as a boy, replied: "No, because I believe that death is like birth. If you had been asked whether you wanted to be born, you would probably have said: 'No, never! Why should I leave my mother's warm womb where I have all the food, nourishment and protection I need?' But if you were never born, you would never have known the exciting adventure of full life as a human being on earth."

Welcome Friend!

What is death? It can be the solution to many problems. This is not meant cynically. At times death comes not as an enemy seeking our destruction, but as a friend liberating us from pain, suffering, even agony.

Death is not always an avenging angel. It can at times be a healing presence, the arrival of a loved and longed-for friend. Death need not be conceived as cold clammy hands poised to rob and terrorize its victims. It can be the soft touch, the gentle look which says: "You are almost home. Here is where you belong."

Death is told not to be proud, and it is well said. But there are other things to say to it:

"Death, be my friend, not my foe. Be my rescuer, my liberator. Death don't take me by surprise. Help me to prepare for your visit. Teach me to live well so that when you come I will greet you as a friend."

● Side Street

Listen to the words of a nurse to the family of a patient who had just died: "Death came with friendly care and touching tenderness. Your mother seemed to fall asleep as peacefully as an infant in her mother's arms."

Death: Natural, yet Absurd

A flower is born to bloom and die. It dies, a seed begins to grow, and another flower appears.

Human death has a similar naturalness. Many people accept death as the end of their lives. The play finished and the final curtain fallen. They have lived full lives, developing their talents and enjoying themselves. They have sought to be and to do their best for their family, community and the world. When death comes, there is an ease and naturalness about it.

The death of a person who has lived a full life may seem quite natural, but other deaths do not. The death of a child, or of a young person vibrant with promise. The death of a parent whose family still needs him or her. The death of a spouse of one or sixty years whose love made marriage a blissful reality.

In such cases, the fact that death is natural offers little consolation and one cries out: "Why my child? My spouse? My friend? Why me?"

For these the death of a human being is an absurd cutting off of a person's consciousness and personal growth. Death leaves so many things still to be done.

Those who do not believe in God may find consolation in philosophy, humanism or the thought that some good has been accomplished even by the youngest person.

Those who have faith in God may seek an answer in that faith. That answer will be comforting or frightening depending upon how they view God.

The Trinity

Do you believe in a God who is three persons, Father, Son and Holy Spirit? How do you relate to that God? Is the Father an authoritarian figure, or a firm, loving parent who enables you to grow?

Is the Son the "Big Brother" with all the overtones which that term has, or is he an older brother who cares for and protects you when you need him? Is the Holy Spirit a forgotten presence, a useless commodity, or an active love sanctifying your life?

If you relate in a positive way to God who is three persons you cannot die alone.

In the act of dying you commit yourself into the loving care of the ideal Father who has never and will never cease to love you. You give yourself to a saving Brother with complete

Why not learn to energize your unique capacity to love by immersing yourself in and reflecting God's perfect love?

faith in his power and desire to protect you on your journey home. Because you believe in a sanctifying Spirit you know that no moment, first or last, eludes his influence.

As a member of the Christian faith community, you are part of the People of God, the Mystical Body of Christ and the Community of the Spirit. "The People of God" signifies a special relationship with the Father toward whom you are journeying as one of his pilgrim people. "The Mystical Body of Christ" means that you are directly united with Jesus Christ and the other members of his body. "The Community of the Spirit" shows that you are part of a people open to the Spirit who lives and works in you.

Your Saintly Family

Another belief which offers comfort is the Communion of the Saints. All those who have gone before you are still united to you, especially the many people whom you have loved and who have loved you.

At the moment of your death, they will undoubtedly find fresh ways to show their love. They will help you by their unseen and often unrealized presence to pass through the portals of the next life.

In a sense, they will be the spiritual midwives at your second birth. Only this time there will be no chance of a mishap. This birth will be normal, healthy, completely successful and joyous. This time you will be born to the fullness of life and the perfection of all your faculties. No childish gibberish, no helpless cries, no harsh lights or sounds to frighten you. Just the complete and mutually rewarding communication with God and your loved ones that you sought, but never quite achieved, here on earth.

Remind yourself of these things, of who you are and to whom you belong. To believe fully in these things is never to be alone in life or in death.

● *Side Street*

The Spirit of Jesus Christ cannot die. If and when we let the Spirit truly be our life, we will possess the fruits of the Spirit—love, joy, peace, patient endurance, kindness, goodness, trustfulness, gentleness and self-control. These qualities bring life, not death.

Death does not touch the Spirit—and it will not touch our spirit except if we refuse to proclaim and to live that we belong to Jesus, who has conquered sin, suffering and death.

"Since we live by the Spirit, let us follow the Spirit's lead" (Gal 5:25). He leads us to new life through our death. The Holy Spirit will be with us at the last moment to sanctify it as he has all the other moments of our life. He will offer us graceful resignation, peaceful acceptance, and a vision of the happiness which will be ours.

Death in Philosophy and Theology

Philosophers and theologians view death as a destruction which befalls all people. Most of us who have seen someone die would readily agree with that description.

Philosophers and theologians also see death as a transition to the form of being that we humans will have after death. Here death is destruction and transition at the same time: a most complete destruction which is apparent, and a transition which is hidden from the eyes of the observers, but not from the eyes of faith.

As the former preface of the funeral Mass proclaimed: "Life is changed, not ended."

This transition is simultaneously the completion of earthly life and the entrance into life after death. It is not something "in between" both, but the real transition, the moment in which a person is changed from the first to the second way of existing. This transition is our birth into a new life.

Death as destruction and transition is at the same time most passive and most active, a fate which befalls us and an action freely chosen.

Death is called an "act" insofar as it is the completion of our own permanent active growth as persons. Death can be called "free" inasmuch as it is the completion of our personal freedom and of all our free decisions.

The Dutch theologian, Schoonenberg, sees death as the totalization and synthesis of our whole life, the fixation of the direction of that life. Death thus becomes the entrance into either a good or bad eternity. He calls the *active* element in dying the eternalization of the direction of our earthly life.

What happens at the moment of death? In seeking answers to that question, some theologians have maintained that a person is frozen exactly where he is in relation to God, the world and other humans.

Other theologians say that it is not so much what a person is at death that counts, although it is important but what counts is the fundamental direction that the individual has given to life, which is ratified at that last moment.

Another group says that in the moment of death a person makes a final decision summing up in a completely free human act all that he was and all that he tried to be. According to this last group, the final decision in death is an *act* although not visible to observers. Methods of determining the exact moment of death are still quite crude so it is not surprising that observers would not know what is going on at that moment.

The decision is *free* because the person making it finally escapes from all the environmental, hereditary and personal influences which inhibited him during life.

The decision is *relative* because the person sums up his relationships with God, with self, with others and the world. He chooses to be with all of these in love. Or he chooses to turn his back on them and live in isolation. If he chooses the latter, then he seeks himself in a completely and everlastingly self-centered way.

The decision is *re-creative* because the person recreates or restructures what type of body he wants for the new life which he is beginning.

Death, which is really birth to a new life, might very well include such a decision. But not everyone accepts this theory. It has some strong points and some weak ones.

Strong Points

It helps us understand how God's love touches each human being. Otherwise we question how God reaches the child who dies in the womb, the "God-forsaken" bum on the Bowery, or the person who has never heard of God. In death, as the final decision is being made, the person has all his faculties working perfectly although this is not apparent to others.

This ultimate activity of life occurs at the deepest levels of being and existence. In that moment of final decision, the person meets his Creator and freely decides how he wants to relate to Him and others. God's love is always available for everyone and in every part of the world. This theory shows how his love touches every human being especially at the last moment.

The final decision also makes more sense of heaven, hell and purgatory. Heaven and hell are not places we are assigned to by God. They are relationships with God and with others that we choose in that final decision. We choose them freely and with full knowledge.

So, if I am in heaven or hell as a result of my final decision, I not only cannot but will not want to change that decision.

It has been suggested that the final decision itself may be purgatory. In that final decision, I break through all the layers of selfishness and finally grow up. I experience something comparable to an instant adolescence. It is an intense process and thus purgatory is measured by its intensity and not by duration of time.

Two of the leading proponents of this theory, Ladislaus

Boros and Robert Gleason, also believe that the final decision is the moment of judgment, not so much by God, but by self. God only ratifies what the person as an individual chooses.

Weak Points

Two objections are usually raised. If there is a final decision at the moment of death, why bother trying to be good? Why not gamble that you will make the right decision at death?

But such an attitude is immature and also risky. The person making the final decision has been formed by the acts of a lifetime. The odds are against any drastic change of direction. If I have been self-centered and vicious all my life, I'll probably decide to remain that way at the moment of death.

The other objection is that the final decision presupposes an angelic morality, not a human morality. Only the angels could possibly decide so utterly and with such complete knowledge. No human being could do the same in this life.

But *in death* this could happen, especially if the person is freed from all determinants. However, the person would not decide as an angel, but as a human being who has lived in history and has been a part of that history.

For Whom

Saints will have no trouble in making the final decision. They will die the way that they have lived. Hardened sinners will probably decide in death just as they decided in their lifetime. They will choose themselves over everyone and everything else.

But the vast majority of people who are neither saints nor sinners will find in this particular decision a real opportunity to clarify and to finalize what they tried to do with their lives.

So there it is—an interesting, comforting but disputed theory. Understood completely and correctly it places great value on what a person does and becomes during life, yet offers a hope of conversion commensurate with God's infinite mercy.

● *Side Street*

"A fundamental principle that must never be forgotten is 'God made the world for His own glory, but He glorifies Himself in this life by His mercy'."

—M. Eugene Boylan

Nature's Answer

After all is said by philosophers and theologians, I still want to know what death is. Is there nothing in my ordinary experience that will help me understand this problem which is also a mystery, this natural yet absurd event?

Have you ever awakened from a deep sleep feeling so rested and refreshed, so completely one with yourself that you knew exactly where you were and what you were doing? You felt so good that you could have stayed there all day and yet, when you realized where you were, you gladly and effortlessly got up and began to do your work? There is some comparison between such a peaceful awakening and death. But be assured that the awakening or transition which takes place in death is much smoother, and far more exhilarating than even the most graceful awakening after a deep soothing sleep.

When we experience the final birth to everlasting life—to our second spring—we will know where we are. We will be as glad to be there as we are to be alive on a beautiful day. We will be perfectly fulfilled and thus completely happy.

But perhaps nature best answers our questions.

Sunrise? Sunset?

Which of the two do you associate with death?

Sunset is such a restful time, quiet and colorful. It eases us into a sleepy mood, gently erasing the cares and woes of the day.

Sunrise is a time for life, motion and activity. It is stirring movement and joyful sound.

Which of the two do you associate with death? You'd be

right if you thought most people associated death with sunset. But you might be surprised at how many people associate death with sunrise. The latter group are Easter people—persons of hope in life which conquers death.

● *Side Street*

Next time you see a sunset, pause and allow its restful but active beauty to embrace you.

Make it a point to see a sunrise soon. It's worth the effort and loss of sleep to see the way creation responds to the birth of a new day. Do you think God will be outdone by his creation when he welcomes you as you are born to your new and everlasting day?

CHAPTER FOUR
TO LIVE AGAIN

Mourn Me

> *Mourn me not with tearful sighs.*
> *Mourn me not with anguished cries.*
> *Mourn me not with undying sorrow.*
> *Mourn me not unceasingly.*
>
> *Mourn me better, mourn me well.*
> *Mourn the passing of physical intimacy,*
> *The touching and talking of our life together.*
> *All the little things which were our happiness.*

Mourn me for awhile. Only for a time.
Let it out for that is good but
As you mourn, know in your heart and mind
I am reborn to a far, far better life.

Build your own life until we meet again.
Rejoice in the unshakeable conviction that
I have not died to love or you.
Our love lives on and conquers death.

Death itself must one day die.
Love alone lives forever.
We together by undying love
Conquer all death and dying.

Love lives on.

Grief and Emotions

How do your emotions affect your understanding of death? You may believe and be convinced intellectually that God is love and that no matter what happens all things will work out for the best. St. Paul reassures us when he says: "We know that God makes all things work together for the good of those who have been called according to his decree" (Rm 8:28).

But when someone we love dies, especially if there has been no warning, our faith is sorely tested. We must fight through darkness and doubts. "I know that God is love. But why don't I feel his love now? I know that Jesus is Lord of the living and the dead, but why do I feel so lost and broken inside"?

Every Christian who has ever loved has faced such a dilemma. It is the problem of integrating what we believe with how we feel, our intellectual life with our emotional life.

Too often we live on only one level. We are ruled by our minds, rigidly controlling our feelings within limits acceptable to our way of thinking. Or we just ride the waves of our emotions and forget about thinking things out. Only when we finally accept ourselves as thinking, feeling persons and seek to understand and feel who and what we are, can we live in wholeness and maturity.

There is a problem for most of us in admitting that sadness and sorrow are just as much a part of our life as joy and happiness. We go to great lengths to deceive ourselves.

When death strikes our loved ones, it tears away our defenses, our efforts at detachment. Death robs us of our masks and forces us to face some unpleasant facts.

No one of us has the complete answer to all the questions death raises. I can just share with you my faith and my limited experiences. Certain truths illuminate our way in moments of sorrow.

You and I are loved and lovable. We are loved by God and by many other persons. We were and are loved by the one for whom we mourn. That love very likely has made us more lovable.

In our time of sorrow, we are the recipient of much attention. Family, friends, and acquaintances assure us that we are not alone. Many times they will not be eloquent. They may not even express such thoughts. They're just there with us.

There was a priest of whom it was said that he never failed to comfort the bereaved. Someone asked him his secret. He replied: "All I do is go up to the person, take her by the hand, look into her eyes and say, 'I'm sorry. I'm truly sorry. I want to help you if I can'."

His words were ordinary but his manner was not. He was not afraid to touch, to look at the person and not away from her. He was eager to share her sorrow, pain and grief and to offer words of comfort.

God must be like that priest, only more so. God so loved the world that he gave his only Son for our redemption. The Son became like us in all things but sin. Death was no stranger to him. He knew it, experienced it and conquered it. He will show us the way through our experience of death. He has been there.

And Yet

Why is it so difficult to express our feelings when someone has died? We mumble formulas, say something—almost anything —that comes to mind, and then hurry away or change the subject. Anything but come to grips with the situation.

This difficulty is nothing new, nor is it limited to visitors. Often the family of the deceased does not know how to handle anything but a very stylized statement of sympathy.

Barriers have been built up over a lifetime, dams which block emotional expressions or feelings. Reluctance to admit the existence of such feelings is heightened by death.

It seems, at least for me, that the best approach is to express my sorrow in my own words no matter how simple and ordinary. A warm sympathetic greeting, a heartfelt prayer, and then a quiet supportive presence means more than many words.

Wakes are not places to linger. Wakes are for communication, verbal and otherwise, with the bereaved. Though difficult, it can be immensely comforting to them and rewarding to us.

Prayerful support and meaningful communication are also needed after the funeral. At that time if you cannot express your feelings verbally in a deep heartfelt way, then do something else. Perhaps a note, letter, card, call, visit, gift. You have a special talent for comforting those in need, a talent as unique as you are. Consider these examples:

> A student, when her best friend's father died, never sent a card or flowers, but spent the whole week with her friend helping in any way she could.

> Some neighbors prepare salads, sandwiches and cake for the family after the funeral.

> A friend lends a helping hand with children who have lost a mother or a father.

> Dan and Helen don't ignore Mary, a recently widowed friend, but assist her from the abundance of their own secure married love.

Remember that the need for consolation does not "go away" in a few days or even weeks. Oftentimes just being a good listener is of inestimable help to the bereaved especially after most other people have forgotten.

● *Side Street*

Chris and Debbie deepened their friendship tremendously after Debbie's father died. As Debbie said: "Chris was the only one of my friends who cared enough, even months after the funeral, to encourage me to talk about my feelings." Caring was the key which unlocked the gates of Debbie's grief. Chris, by caring, halved that lonely burden.

Wakes

Whether or not you agree with wakes as they are customarily held is a personal matter, but it might be helpful to sort out your feelings. One day you may have to decide if and how a wake will be conducted for you or a loved one. Right now your only decision may well be whether or not to attend the wake of a friend or relative.

Participate in the efforts to console the survivors by your presence. And, in addition to supportive words and gestures, simply pray. Pray on the way to and from the wake. Begin with your favorite prayer. Say it once for the deceased, and another for each of the relatives and survivors. Then continue to pray as the Holy Spirit leads you. Mention your prayers to the family. They will be deeply touched by your loving concern.

A spray of flowers thoughtfully chosen by the family adds natural beauty to the occasion and may symbolize special memories or interests of the deceased. An abundance of flowers detracts from the special meaning of the family bouquet and is also an unnecessary expense.

Today more people are asking that flowers be replaced by donations in the name of the deceased to medical science, charitable institutions or other organizations which help the living.

● *Side Street*

A quite unoriginal thought: "Don't wait until they're dead to do something nice for them."

The *usual* response: "I really must do something when I get the time."

A most *unusual* response: "*I will do it now, this day, this moment.*"

The usual self-justification for delay: "I'm too busy right now. Maybe tomorrow." A possible reply: "How many tomorrows do I have?"

How long does it take to call someone, to write a short note, to send flowers? If you work twelve hours a day there are still twelve left. Fifteen minutes of one of those hours is all it takes. If you can't find the time, do one of two things.

1. Check your will, say your prayers and get ready. You're running out of time and that means *you* are closer to death than you imagine.

2. MAKE THE TIME!

Death Reveals Goodness

I think of a woman, by nature gracious, kind and considerate, a born teacher. She had always been a blessed presence to her students and associates, but even greater was her impact when struck by cancer.

Painful treatments and long months of suffering altered her physical appearance, yet seemed only to intensify her loving concern for others.

When she died, friends and students both past and present gathered to pay their respects. They sought to console her family. They failed.

Instead, from their abundant faith, the family gave comfort and encouragement to all who came.

For some of her students it was their first wake and sincerity did not conceal their awkward sorrow and shock at seeing how the cancer had ravished her body. Groping for words they self-consciously approached her parents who thanked them warmly for their thoughtfulness to their daughter and themselves. The parents proved many things by their words and actions. They mourned with quiet joy, turned awkward silences into tenderness.

The dead woman had been a Dominican Sister. She had learned much in her life as a religious, but had also brought much to it. Her parents were living proof of that. All three are unforgettable people—Sister because of the way she lived and died; her parents because of the way they mourned and lived.

● *Side Street*

Personal existence is always greater than words can express. No words can ever exhaust the mystery of being a person.

Sometimes death alone reveals the true nature of a person. Stories are recounted, incidents recalled, anecdotes related, which provide rare glimpses into a person's life. People acknowledge what the dead person has meant to them at crucial moments of their lives. Our Western reluctance to use praise except in the smallest doses seems to dissolve when the person can no longer "get a big head."

Why not be a little more generous in your praise! Give it when the recipient can still appreciate it.

Celebrating the Eucharist

A funeral Mass which is planned and celebrated well can be a great consolation and a time of grace for all who participate in it. If at all possible, the family and friends of the deceased should be invited to share in the planning and celebration of the liturgy. At times a dying person will express a wish for certain readings or hymns. Planning one's own funeral liturgy may sound strange, but it can be a surprisingly consoling faith experience.

Joyful symbols abound in the funeral liturgy. The vestments are white which is symbolic of the Resurrection. Often a green trim is used because the color signifies new life and hope, a second spring. The paschal candle represents the light of Christ shining for us in life and death.

The opening prayer may speak about God's everlasting mercy refreshing the person and admitting him to the fellowship of the saints.* We may also ask God to let the deceased "share the glory of the risen Christ," to grant him the freedom of perfect peace, and to give him the unending joy of love which will bring light, happiness and peace.

---

*All references are to *The New Sacramentary* (New York, 1974) Catholic Book Publishing Co.

There is a beautiful opening prayer on the anniversary of a person's death.

> "Lord God, you are the glory of
> believers and the life of the just.
> Your son redeemed us by dying and
> rising to life again.
> Our brother (sister) was faithful
> and believed in our own resurrection.
> Give to him (her) the joys and blessings
> of the life to come."

The readings from Scripture take on an unusual force and meaning especially if they have a particular relevance to the deceased. The living and dynamic Word of God helps us to penetrate the mystery of death.

The homily has a special impact. The celebrant offers comfort, quiet hope and deep sympathy. He highlights the message of resurrection—faith in a God whose love is stronger than death. In a few sentences, he tries to show how the dead person lived the Christian life and what lessons she or he taught us.

But the emphasis is on understanding and accepting the consolation and comfort of God's Word. All eyes should be fixed on the Risen Savior who alone knows our deepest feelings. Jesus is truly the *Way*, the *Truth*, and the *Life* we seek at such moments.

Prefaces for Christian Death

The beauty and variety of the prefaces for Christian death should be a source of great comfort and joy, but we need time to understand them and think about them. Each preface is addressed to the Father and recalls what Jesus has done.

Preface I

"Father, all powerful and ever-living God, we do well always and everywhere to give you thanks, through Jesus Christ our

Lord. In him, who rose from the dead, our hope of resurrection dawned. The sadness of death gives way to the bright promise of immortality.

Lord, for your faithful people life is changed, not ended. When the body of our earthly dwelling lies in death we gain an everlasting dwelling place in heaven."

Preface II

"He (Christ) chose to die that he might free all men from dying. He gave his life that we might live to you (Father) alone forever."

Preface III

"In him (Christ) the world is saved, man is reborn, and the dead rise again to life."

Preface IV

"By your power you bring us to birth.
By your providence you rule our lives.
By your command you free us at last from sin
As we return to the dust from which we came.
Through the saving death of your Son
We rise at your word to the glory of the resurrection."

Preface V

"Death is the just reward for our sins, yet, when
at last we die, your loving kindness calls us back
to life in company with Christ, whose victory is our redemption."

Acclamations

After the consecration of the Mass we acclaim Christ's victory over death.

"Christ has died,

Christ is risen,
Christ will come again."

"Dying you destroyed our death,
rising you restored our life,
Lord Jesus come in glory."

The Eucharistic prayers of the Mass always refer to the death and resurrection of Jesus Christ and often link his death with ours. One of the most beautiful is the third Eucharistic prayer, often used in funeral liturgies. It proclaims:

"Remember (name of deceased). In baptism he died with Christ, may he also share his resurrection when Christ will raise our mortal bodies and make them like his own in glory. Welcome into your kingdom our departed brothers and sisters and all who have left this world in your friendship. There we hope to share in your glory when every tear will be wiped away. On that day we shall see you, our God, as you are. We shall become like you and praise you forever through Christ our Lord, from whom all good things come."

A Personal Note

My father died in 1968 just after I had finished the Good Friday services. It was a shock, but not a complete surprise since he had a heart condition. I left immediately to be with my mother and family.

The sisters of the community which I serve as chaplain made it clear that they would understand if I decided not to come back for the Easter Vigil Service. I did return. Several people remarked how considerate that was. A nice thought, but not true.

At that time I needed to celebrate the Mass of the Resurrection in a beautiful liturgical setting with the full participation of a prayerful community. My faith needed to be renewed in Jesus Christ, my risen Lord, who is the light of the world and the light of all of our lives. I believe in the Resurrection but that was not enough. I had to be plunged liturgically into the reality of Easter joy. I needed it, wanted it, and found tremendous consolation in it.

"We are Easter People—Alleluia" were not new words to me, but in those circumstances they took on a new significance. The Easter candle, the alleluias, the bells as they echoed through the church made the Easter Vigil Service and Mass an unforgettable experience. That Easter touched the core of my being and remained with me throughout the days of mourning. I hope never to forget it.

Regrets

Has someone you loved died? What was your reaction after the initial shock? "I'm so glad I could be there and provide for all his or her needs."

Unfortunately, few of us seem to react that way. Often we think, "Why wasn't I nicer? Why didn't I visit more often or at least call every day?" We are not speaking of heartless, uncaring individuals here, but of normal, loving people.

Perhaps a story will help. One woman, with a large family of her own, cared for her blind and invalid mother for years. The care she gave her mother with the greatest affection was beyond any price. And yet, when her mother died, the daughter wished that she had been nicer. Why had she insisted that her mother take her medicine, refused to give her foods that were not on her diet, or forced her to do things for her own good? I immediately seized upon the expression "for her own good" and said that everything the daughter had done, as far as I knew, had been done for the mother's good. How few could have loved a parent as well as she had.

The first pangs of grief, regret and recrimination strike all except the most hardened souls.

Do not lose your sense of perspective. Take time and listen

"The Resurrection is the answer."

to your mind as well as your heart and to the opinions of others who knew the situation. If you tried to do your best or close to it, be at peace.

If you should have been more loving and concerned, then make amends. Tell your loved one that you are sorry. Learn how to value the family and friends you still have. Do good in the name of the deceased.

Do not be too hard on yourself. Your very sense of regret proves something. You were probably more sensitive to the needs of the dying person than you now realize.

The Nagging "If"

"If I had only been there, my child would still be alive and healthy."

"If I had treated my teenager better, he might never have died of an overdose of drugs."

We can linger only so long on the past. It can and does teach many a valuable lesson. But once such knowledge has been gained, the past must be left to the past. Now it's time to live in the present and plan for the future.

Good advice. Putting it into practice is hard. Nonetheless, it must be done.

The greatest consolation of our faith is that God is a loving father. It is on his loving mercy that we throw ourselves when we have sinned, failed or been unkind. We trust in the Father who loves and comforts all—both the living and the dead. When we can no longer say "I'm sorry" to the offended person face to face, we ask our Father to do it.

Survivors: A New Role

The mother of a teenage boy killed in an automobile accident once wrote, "Please pray for the speedy recovery of the survivors." Perhaps some of these suggestions will help that recovery.

"Bow humbly under God's mighty hand so that in due time

he may lift you high. Cast all your cares on him because he *cares
for you*" (1 P 5:6-7).

The survivors can do many things for the deceased. First,
pray for the dead and, if necessary, ask their forgiveness.

Try to rectify the wrongs that the deceased may have in-
flicted on others while alive. Why? The people who were
wronged will appreciate it. You, the survivors, will feel better.
The deceased would quite likely want to do it now if he could.

Guidance from the Dead

> Though I have died and left you here awhile,
> Watch not in lonely sorrow by my grave.
> Rather turn again to life and smile for me,
> Nerving yourself to comfort those in need.
> As you perform such loving acts,
> Do so in my name and yours.
> And find therein both love and comfort.

The Dead Help the Living

Organ transplants have restored many people to health. Another group which has benefited is the donor's surviving relatives. They are justifiably proud that the person they loved was
noble enough to help others live by donating his or her organs.

Many lives can be saved, health and sight can be restored to
thousands if we make arrangements now to donate our organs,
tissues, and/or corneas to those in desperate need of them.

Uniform donor cards are available from the Continental
Association of Funeral and Memorial Societies, 1828 L Street,
N.W., Washington, D. C. 20036 or from local memorial societies.
We can sometimes be the principal stumbling block in refusing
life to others. If we complete a donor card ourselves, we can
spare our families the painful decision they may be asked to make
if we die without making our intentions or desires known.

A valiant woman was faced with such a decision when her
husband had a massive stroke. After all medical efforts had failed

to revive him, she was asked to donate his kidneys to two patients who needed such transplants. Her affirmative answer came easily because she knew that the husband would have done it himself if he were able.

Her response really surprised no one who knew her or her husband because they were both such giving people. She lives now content with her decision and the knowledge that others are alive today because of her "Yes."

I remember driving with some friends to her husband's wake and hearing over the radio that a kidney transplant operation had just been successfully performed in a neighboring state and that the donor had been a man who had died in our nearby hospital.

A coincidence? Perhaps. A comfort? Definitely. The news of the successful transplant lightened the burden of her grief.

Because of her heightened awareness of the need for organ donors, she has recently completed a uniform donor card and proudly carries it with her. She laughingly remarks that when she meets her husband in heaven, she doesn't want him to kid her: "You freely gave away my kidneys, what about your own"?

She has decided that her most precious gift to some as yet unknown member of God's family will be part of herself.

Joyful Words from Survivors to Those Who Cared

"Thank you for your prayers—and sing the alleluia."

"The Lord has blessed us with such good friends near and far. It was a comfort to hear his message through you. We value you because you're you."

"Dad is happily united with the Lord. Through our tears we can smile. Please keep in touch."

" 'Happy now are the dead who die in the Lord; Yes, they shall find rest from their labors, for their good works accompany them' " (Rv 14:13).

"This is the faith that sustains us. You have reinforced that belief by your words, a visit, your note, a promise of Masses and prayers—your joining with us in the celebration of the funeral Mass."

"Mother lived a life such as to encourage trust in God. We are grateful to her, to you and to God."

Eternal Rest or Eternal Life

"Eternal rest" is a verbal image of the future life. If we are exhausted by living, by working to support a family, by caring for sick parents or children, then eternal rest is very appealing. For others of us "eternal life" is a more attractive description of heaven. Eternal life may be seen as active and joyful pursuit of learning, loving and growing. It means developing all the talents and potentialities we have as individuals. Eternal life means the actualization of all the things that we left undone or just talked about in this life.

"Eternal rest" and "eternal life" are human words to describe a far superior reality. Heaven will certainly be a state of rest and solitude even better than what we sought, but rarely achieved, on earth. However, it will also be a state of peaceful activity. The hectic pursuit of goals will be over, but in its place will be the quiet natural achievement of all that we want to be. Actually heaven may be described as both eternal rest and eternal life. The consoling thing about both phrases is that they scarcely describe the reality.

It is good to realize that not everything ends at death. Rather everything good gets better. After death we continue to develop and grow. We are brought into the presence of almighty God to live with him forever. We are limited vessels but our capacity is everlastingly expandable.

Our capacity to know, to love and to enjoy God expands effortlessly and endlessly. There is never any feeling of frustration, emptiness, or futility. In a very natural way we continue to know and enjoy more of God and his love. That really is heaven no matter what name we use for it.

You Will Live Forever: Immortality

For some people death is the end of everything. But for most of us there is some form of immortality after death. The word, however, has many meanings.

There is personal and biological as well as generational and monumental immortality. These are different levels of the same reality and several forms of immortality can be achieved by one person.

Biological immortality means that you live on in your physical descendants. These will hopefully bear more resemblance than just a shared name or some physical characteristics. You may achieve partial biological immortality by donating your body to science, or giving your organs to those who need them to survive.

Generational immortality is comforting to the childless, although available as well to those with children. In this type you are concerned for the next generation and desire to leave behind something positive and permanent for them to treasure and develop. With every particle of your being, you want to express the things which you have felt, and to achieve the goals you have sought during your lifetime.

Monumental immortality is sought in empires and conglomerates, in brick and mortar, in statues or buildings with one's name on them.

Immortality is personal when the "I" which the person has become during life survives death and lives on in some form. Christian tradition proclaims that the person's "life is changed, not ended. When the body of our earthly dwelling lies in death, we gain an everlasting dwelling place in heaven" (Preface of Christian Death I).

Immortality is continuity of life not in the identical form

as before, but in different forms and on various levels—personal, biological, generational and maybe even monumental.

You and I can and will have personal immortality and some of the other forms. But it cannot be put off until later. Whatever immortality we want, we must begin to seek it now.

Let us love and cherish our children as messengers to another age. We should build so that our monuments will last. Monuments in stone are good if they serve the human race, but more meaningful monuments may be built by acts of kindness and concern, or expressed in works of genius or compassion.

● Side Street

If you had only 24 hours to live, what would you do?

Your answer reveals much about you and your values.

Whatever that answer is, maybe you ought to start putting it into practice right now, if you are not already doing it.

I used to think I'd contently answer the question above by saying: "Just the normal things I do each day." Besides being almost intolerably smug, the answer wasn't even close to the mark. If I had only 24 hours to live, I'd spend some hours with my family whom I love dearly. Then I'd celebrate a very long, relaxed and reverent Mass with the community of believers who minister to me as I attempt to minister to them. Afterwards I'd go to my favorite spot on the Jersey shore and again enjoy my Lord's gifts of sun and sand and surf.

The final hours would be spent in the chapel at my seashore retreat. It is a place where I have often met my Lord before. I'd like him to find me waiting there in familiar surroundings. But this time I'm sure I would be more anxious than ever to feel his loving presence and embrace.

The Resurrection

The Resurrection is much more than an empty tomb.

The Resurrection is the risen Jesus, aglow with life, glorious in his victory over suffering and death.

The Resurrection is Mary Magdalene blinded by tears and sorrow, unconsoled by an empty tomb, uncomprehending of the angel's words. It is Mary Magdalene suddenly restored to sight and joy by one word from a man she thought a gardener, the risen Jesus who with tender love says "Mary." Jesus, her Lord, is not dead. He lives and loves her still.

The Resurrection is a race between Peter and John to an empty tomb, but even more to the beginning of a deeper understanding of the Lord of life and death.

The Resurrection is a walk in desolation to Emmaus, a walk suddenly changed into a glorious encounter with a strangely captivating man who made the Scripture come alive as never before. The Resurrection is a race from Emmaus to Jerusalem by two men aglow with renewed faith. They have seen, heard, talked and been fed in many ways by their risen Jesus.

The Resurrection is Jesus loving the doubting Thomas from, "I'll never believe," to the great act of belief and adoration, "My Lord and my God."

It is the risen Jesus, bringing peace and promising his Holy Spirit to renew and rejuvenate his followers.

The Resurrection is Jesus with Mary, his mother, in an unrecorded embrace of love and comfort after her bitter torment and trial. It is a reward for faith sorely tested but never quenched. It is a Son's concern for his sorrowing mother, a word to guide her as she prepares to shepherd his frightened shepherds, as she once more prepares to give birth to his body, now his Church.

The Resurrection is the answer to any doubt about whether God could and would do it. He never counts the cost. Did he not give his son to suffer and die for our sins? The Resurrection and Ascension of Jesus was the Father's final approbation of all that his son had done. The Resurrection and the Ascension taken together echo the Father's word, "You are truly my beloved son in whom I am well pleased. You have done all the many things that I have asked of you. Come home now."

The Resurrection is not words, feelings, speculations, argumentation or controversy. The Resurrection is belief beyond words, joy unknown, faith not in an empty tomb but in a God who is love and life.

There are many things about the Resurrection of Jesus and our own resurrection that we do not understand. Saint Paul tells us that Jesus has truly risen from the dead. If it were not so, we would be the most unfortunate of people. But Jesus has risen from the dead and we too one day will share his resurrection. Consequently, we are not the most unfortunate of people, but by far the *most fortunate.* (See 1 Cor 15:12-23)

A Prayer

Jesus, risen Lord, let the power of your risen humanity fill our lives so that we may conquer all fear of death and sin. Teach us to live in the glory of your unending life.

Heaven

How do you describe the indescribable? What words are there for heaven? "Eye has not seen, ear has not heard, nor has it so much as dawned on man what God has prepared for those who love him" (1 Cor 2:9).

Heaven is our goal, for it is our real home. Heaven is ignored too often and by too many people. So we must try to understand more about it.

Let us begin knowing that we'll fall far short of the reality but learn much even as we fail.

Heaven is the end of the road, and being "Home at last, home at last, thank God Almighty, I'm home at last."

Heaven is the acceptance of our finitude and God's infinity. Heaven is a hunger to enjoy the immensity of God—but without hunger pangs.

Heaven is growth in the knowledge and love of God, but without effort. Heaven is living calmly and confidently without fear of anyone or anything.

Heaven is God and, since we will never exhaust the mystery of God, we will never exhaust the wonder of heaven. Heaven is contentment and great delight because God is inexhaustible and thus heaven will never end.

Heaven is freedom from fear and frustration, joy without resentment.

Heaven is finally understanding why God could and did love us, could and did save us; for in heaven we will see how he is love beyond all our hopes and expectations and how we are and *were* truly lovable even in the depths of our own sins.

Heaven is that state of being where we are totally known for who we are, and where we are totally loved with the infinite passion of God himself. There our spirit finds peace and fulfillment.

Heaven is you and I facing each other and fearlessly saying, "Friend." Heaven is warmth and light and love and all else that makes living joyous.

Heaven is the presence of loved ones, the absence of rancor and wrath.

Heaven is God and home, a song and a poem, a life without death, a joy in the depths of our being. Heaven is the unshakable conviction that we are loved. Heaven is simple pure praise that will never end but will refresh and delight us always.

Heaven is freedom *to be* "me" at last, the real "me" so often obscured during life. Heaven is freedom *for* loving and being loved by all. Heaven is freedom from sin and death, *from* every evil and all life-destroying restrictions. Heaven is all these and yet, after all is said, we must admit that we've only just begun.

● *Side Street*

Read some biblical passages which describe heavenly worship.

". . . I saw the Lord seated on a high and lofty throne, with the train of his garment filling the temple. Seraphim were stationed above . . .

'Holy, Holy, Holy is the Lord of hosts' they cried one to the other. 'All the earth is filled with his glory!' "

"At the sound of that cry, the frame of the door shook and the house was filled with smoke" (Is 6:1-4).

"Day and night, without pause, they sing: 'Holy, holy, holy, is the Lord God Almighty, He who was, and who is, and who is to come!' Whenever these creatures give glory and honor and praise to the One seated on the throne, who lives forever and ever, the twenty-four elders fall down before the One seated on the throne, and worship him who lives forever and ever. They throw down their crowns before the throne and sing:

> 'O Lord our God, you are worthy
> to receive glory and honor and power!
> For you have created all things;
> by your will they came to be and
> were made' " (Rv 4:8b-11)!

● *Side Street*

Marriage and Heaven

A marriage where love flourishes, where two people grow and develop deep trust, face problems together and fill each other's needs is a foretaste of heaven.

Such a marriage is a prefigurement of heaven because in it husband and wife mingle their bodies, souls and spirits and for a moment bridge the fear and loneliness which are so much a part of being human. Their striving toward oneness is among the best examples of what our union with God will be in heaven. And yet, even such a marriage pales before the reality of what heaven is.

Communitas Pacis

In this life we have sought certain things—creativity, affection, love, community, and so on. In the life to which we are born by death we will seek similar but deeper ones.

The community which we knew on earth was based on love, race, relationship, culture, age or common interests. Who knows what elements will constitute community in the next life? Certainly they will be broader and more inclusive than the elements just enumerated. All of these elements and more will make up *communitas pacis*, the community of peace, which is heaven.

Hell

Hell is the everlasting negative.

Hell is not heaven, not God, not love, nor warmth nor anything good. Hell is not heaven and that is why it is hell. Hell is night with no hope of day, freezing coldness with no hint of warmth. Hell is you or I alone, unloving and unwilling to love.

Hell is knowing that I am loved and made for love but refusing to be loved. Hell was and is my decision, my turning away from God and others.

Hell is isolation self-imposed in the face of God's unending call to live with him and his family.

Hell, like heaven, is a relationship freely chosen with God, self, others and the world. Hell and heaven are probably not places, but if they were, they might be the same place. The only difference is the difference between night and day, darkness and light, love and hate, joy and self-imposed sorrow.

Theologian John Macquarrie speaks of hell as self-restriction and self-constriction. If people are in hell, they willed to be there, willed to restrict and constrict themselves within the bonds of hate and selfishness. It wasn't and isn't and could never be God's choice. It was and is and always will be their choice and no one else's.

Hell is bondage to selfishness and fear, to rootlessness and loss, to anguish and frustration. Hell is slavery to the devil and the demons so often denied and laughed at during life.

Pictures of hell are never pretty. The reality—to be totally alone forever—is far worse.

Cemeteries: Friendly Or Frightening?

In the sunlight, a cemetery has a special beauty. Green grass, neat rows of headstones, lovely flowers and the clear blue sky create a sense of peace and quiet, a gentle but pervasive presence hard to identify, but nonetheless real.

In such a setting "eternal rest" takes on new meaning. It is no longer just a comforting phrase to be resurrected when the occasion warrants.

Darkness can transform a cemetery most alarmingly. Goose pimples, quivering in the limbs, and other signs of physical and emotional distress often accompany a visit to a darkened cemetery. Subconsciously many of us feel that the dead have not lost all power over us. Could this be a glimmer of our often forgotten belief in immortality? Perhaps more than we want to admit is felt, if not seen, among the darkened monuments.

My Favorite

Nestled in a tree-lined section of the college where I teach is a cemetery in which are buried the deceased members of the Dominican Sisters of Caldwell.

It is a lovely spot, surrounded by hedges which heighten the sense of peace and isolation from the world. Rugged stations of the cross border its path and a crucifix rises from a mound of stones at the heart of this resting place. Flat stone plaques proclaim the basic facts about the sisters buried there.

Walking alone or with another in that place at any time of day or night is an uniquely peaceful experience.

Once on a bright sun-filled day, I celebrated the Eucharist there with some of the sisters. We felt we could almost touch the past because of our kinship with the valiant women who had literally built everything in sight.

I've walked there, talked there, and just been there in prayerful silence, and in playful reverie imagined what tales the dead might tell.

One can feel at ease in that place and know no fear. It is

familiar, light, joyful and surrounded by a large educational institution aglow with life and youth.

One hot September day during Freshmen Orientation, I casually mentioned that we might find it more pleasant to finish our discussions outside in the cool shade of the cemetery. You might imagine the reactions.

However, we did go there, sat on the stone benches and the ground, and had a delightful exchange of ideas. There was no fear, only the peaceful noisiness of an autumn afternoon.

Your local cemetery might be similar, a treasured spot for contemplation and relaxation. If you have an occasion to visit a cemetery, stop for a moment and let yourself become aware of its peacefulness. We who react to death with such mixed emotions have much to learn from those who seem to be dead but are living life to the fullest.

Poetry in an Unexpected Place

Tombstones were once the most popular setting for poetry. Simple words and phrases captured for future generations the life and personality of the deceased, how they viewed life and death, their fortune and misfortune, virtues, vices and eccentricities. There was humor, penetrating insights, lively comments and words of wisdom about life in general.

Have you seen any poetry on modern tombstones? Today there's merely a name, date of birth and death, and sometimes a quotation from Scripture or a religious symbol.

It's as though we have no time for such things and our modern fear of death urges us to get in and out of cemeteries as fast as possible. Perhaps one of today's challenges could be to break the bonds of bland conformity and restore poetry to an unusual but not inappropriate place.

Let the Stones Speak for Themselves

I. *"She's not here ... She's gone home."*

The stones speak.

II.   *"Here lies Mary, the wife of John Ford*
      We hope her soul is gone to the Lord:
      But if for hell she has chang'd this life
      She had better be there than be John Ford's wife."

III.   *"Life's railway o'er, each station passed,*
      In death I'm stopped, and rest at last,
      Farewell, dear friends, and cease to weep:
      In Christ I'm safe: In Him I sleep."
      (On the tomb of a railroad engineer)

IV.   *"Think my dear friends as you pass by*
      As you are now so once was I,
      As I am now so you must be,
      Prepare for death and follow me."

V.   *"Weep not for me, my friends most dear,*
      To grieve it is in vain,
      Christ is my hope, you need not fear,
      We all shall meet again.
      Oh, prepare, prepare to die."

VI.   *"Mourn not, my friends, I feel no more the smart,*
      Of the afflicted head or aching heart:
      Mourn for your sins against a gracious God,
      Believe in Christ and feel his Precious Blood,
      This stone is witness that the warning's given,
      Choose the good part and follow me to Heaven."

VII.   *"Mourn not for me, my parents dear,*
      I am not dead but sleeping here:
      For I am on my Saviour's breast,
      Children He did forever bless."
      (On the tomb of a child)

● *Side Streets*

In certain values clarification sessions each person is asked to write a three-word epitaph. Rather a frightening task isn't it, to decide which three words sum up your life. Consider some possibilities: *"Christian, Father, Friend"; "She Always Cared"; "Never Too Busy"; "Woman of Hope"; "Gentle, Loving, Aware."*

Composing an epitaph for oneself has value. It is good to examine life and find out what makes it important.

Write your own obituary. Date, cause, everything. Did you die too soon, or too late, too suddenly or at the right time? It's a game now but someday a person, other than you, will have the task.

Make it easy, even edifying, for him. Be the best person you can possibly be.

Epilogue

How will you react to death now that you have finished reading this book? Will you be able to face death without any fear? Will the right words come to you automatically when you want to express sympathy? Will you always be able to comfort and console others? Will your faith invariably answer all your questions and needs?

Quite simply, "No."

You will still fear. You will still grope for meaning in the face of death, and search for the right words to express the sympathy that is in your heart. You will still give and receive consolation in a self-conscious manner.

But—and it's a big "but"—you should have less fear of death because you will have confronted it under many aspects. You will, I hope, have achieved an empathy and compassion for other people that you will express not just in words but in your every act. Your very being will be expressive of your sympathetic understanding.

I hope that you will have new insights, and that these will help you to be a better person. I hope that you will return to these pages especially when those close to you or you yourself move closer to that second birth we will probably continue to call death.

I hope that you will then find new meaning in these words and pictures and know something of that not-so-far-distant country through which we all must pass as we are born again and finally complete the journey to our Father's house.

May we learn to accept the love of our Father as he offers us his arms in a loving embrace during life, in death and at our final home.

"Praised be the God and Father of our Lord Jesus Christ, he who in his great mercy gave us a new birth, a birth unto hope which draws its life from the resurrection of Jesus Christ from the dead, a birth to an imperishable inheritance . . . a birth to a salvation which stands ready to be revealed in the last days.

"There is cause for rejoicing here. You may for a time have to suffer the distress of many trials; but this is so that your faith, which is more precious than the passing splendors of fire-tried gold, may by its genuineness lead to praise, glory and honor when Jesus Christ appears" (1 P 1:3-7).